FAITH COMES BY HEARING

SCIENCE COMES BY SEEING

FAITH COMES BY HEARING

SCIENCE COMES BY SEEING

THE FOUR BEGINNINGS: ANGELICAL, COSMOLOGICAL, GEOLOGICAL, AND BIOLOGICAL

BY

NAOMI ELIZABETH PEETE

FOREWORD BY DR. ROBERT L. MANAWAY, SR

Faith comes by Hearing. Science come by Seeing
Copyright © 2017
Published by 'Write It Down. Make It Plain'
Seattle, Washington
ISBN: 978-1-933133-88-1

All Scripture quotations, unless otherwise indicated, are taken from the *Holy Bibles: New International Version (NIV)* ©1973,1978,1984 by International Bible Society; *King James Version (KJV)*. All rights reserved/

All rights reserved. No part of this book may be reproduced, stored in a retrieval system, or transmitted in any form or by any means – electronic, mechanical, photocopy, recording, or otherwise –without permission of the publisher, except for brief quotations in printed reviews.

Printed in the United States of America

Table of Content

> "I will meditate on your precepts and reflect on your ways. I will delight in your decrees and not neglect your word." Psalm 119: 15 – 16

Acknowledgements and Dedications	vii
Foreword by Dr. Robert L. Manaway	ix
Chapter 1: The Bible is not a Science Book	**1-8**
Test all things hold fast what is good	2
Science emerges through the Scriptures	3
Think on these things	4-7
Chapter 2: Discover Science	**9-25**
Biblical Women were STEM-skilled	10
Personal connections to Faith and Science	11
The Chemistry of Baking a Cake with Grandma Sarah	14
Grandma's hands	20
Science behind a woodstove: Thermodynamics	22
Grandma Peete's loving hands	23
Let's Cook Biscuits	24
Chapter 3: Searching the Scriptures	**27-42**
Faith comes by Hearing. Science comes by Seeing. What did they see?	28
In the beginning God Created	32
Examining the Scriptures	36
Abracadabra: creating nothingness into something	37
Celestial Beings- Life in the Universe	38
Chapter 4: Unquenchable Energy on the move	**43-58**
Cosmic time – Big Bang or a Big Bam	44
Reading the signs in the sky	45
Big Bang – Age of Radiation	47
Properties of visual light	49
Earth's Geological timescale	52
How did water come to Earth?	54
Our world dark with emptiness	55
Scientific evidence of meteorites impact	56
Chapter 5: Earth's Nuclear Winter	**59-64**
Trouble in heaven	60
Names of Satan	61
Faster than a speeding bullet-Speed of Angels	62
Chapter 6: Renew, Restore, Replenish	**65**
Day One – Setting off Spiritual Dynamite	**66-81**
Nuclear Winter	66
Brooding and Hovering over the Deep	67
The Ocean and mixing the Primordial Soup	69
Organic Elements of Life	70
God speaks – It happens!	71
Conversation with Talking Animals	72
God Puffs into Adam	73
Time began – Let there be Light!	78
Day Two: Restoration of the Heavens	**82-87**
The Atmosphere- First Heaven	83
Puffy white clouds	83
Second Heaven	87
Third Heaven	87
Day Three: Restoration of the Seas and the Land	**88-107**
Important properties of water	90
Meteorological phenomena – effects of water on the Earth's surface and Atmosphere	90
Start of the longest rain recorded in the Bible	91
Shaking and quaking from fault lines	93
Surveying the landforms	96
Colonization of the land	98
importance of plants	98
plant diversity	99
seeds	99
herbs	102
grasses	102
flowers	102
fruit production	103
trees	104
the rod that sprouted, budded, blossomed, and produced fruit overnight	105
Nature's Orchestra: branches, twigs, leaves, and the wind	106

Day Four: Lights in the Great Sky   **108-114**

     Earth's Yellow Star: The Sun   108
     The Moon   112
     Twinkle, twinkle little Star   114

Day Five: Animals – Creeping, Crawling, Flying, Leaping, Swimming Things   **115-127**

     Restorative conditions provided Sustainability to Earth   115
     Microorganisms: it's a small world after all   117
     God loves Animals and He Blessed them   118
     Animals as our first teachers   119
     Animals used in miraculous ways   120
     Animals as Pets   120
     Survey of the Animal Kingdom   121

Day Six: Large Animals and Humanity Created   **128-137**

     Volcano Eruption: the source of dust   129
     Atmospheric circulation and distribution of soil   130
     The Color of Soil   131
     Establishing the Foundation of Life   133
     Time-line: Connecting Inorganic and Organic Components   136

II. Adam: The Original Template   **138-147**

     The Puff-Respiration   138
     Cardiopulmonary Resuscitation – CPR   139
     Organization within Adam   141
         symmetry   141
         framework   142
         blood   144
         flesh of my flesh   147

III. Eve – The Mother of all living beings   **148-156**

     Purpose of a Help-mate   148
     The Biology of a Woman: **XX** Chromosomes   149
     Eve: created from Stem Cells extraction   149
     There is a little Eve in all of us   151
         Hormones   151
         Eve's skeletal framework   152
         Eve developed more fat cells than Adam-Curves   152
         Eve- the thinking woman's brain   152
         relationship and community   154

Educate to Innovate   **157-159**

STEM-*Science, Technology, Engineering, Mathematics* Matters   **160-161**

Appendix

     Study Guide   163-169
     Resource list   170-171
     About the Author   172

Acknowledgment

To my Kingdom Kids

Okang   Kiana   Malik   Kobe   Keira

and all inquisitive explorers of nature

Dedication

This book is dedicated to the memories of my parents and maternal grandparents, the Late Elder Eddie Peete, Jr. and Ruth Edna Peete and Bishop Robert Clarence and Sarah Handshaw-Butts. Their support, knowledge, encouragement was instrumental in developing my faith and my love of science. They instilled in me by example, a strong sense of discipline and integrity, for which I am eternally grateful.

I further extend grateful appreciation to my family, especially my children Herb, Maurice, Michelle; TCPM Author's group; and many friends for reviewing the manuscript; providing biblical and historical information; offering evidence and insights in science and much prayers.

Lastly, special acknowledgment and thanks to my youngest brother, Stanley Thomas Peete, who shared my passion for the Sciences and Faith. He faithfully challenged me with great wisdom, hard riddles, probing questions, and exegesis of the scriptures while simultaneously applying spiritual content. I learned to go deeper and was amazed at greater truths of Science that can be found in the Bible.

FOREWORD

This book is an exceptional rending of hours of studying the Word of God and relating it to the natural world. It offers compelling explanations as to how science and biblical truth align to explain natural and spiritual truths.

This book is unique in the manner Dr. Peete systematically walks readers through the Bible to show how science affirms the errant Word of God. Further, Dr. Peete skillfully marries, biology, chemistry, botany, and faith to illustrate the wonder of our sovereign God. The book is full of interesting details and references, which are referenced in appropriate photos and captions.

Still further, Dr. Peete shares her extensive knowledge about the subject she presents in this book. As you read the book, you will undoubtedly be impressed by her use of common scholarly reflections to enhance the novice within the inquisitive reader. I admire her skills to interweave faith and science throughout the book.

Each chapter clearly lays out what the reader can expect, which allows you to easily follow the progression of each topic presented. Dr. Peete's uses personal stories and recipes to illustrate the everyday impact science played in her early life that then allowed her to become the observant scholar she would become. The use of such narratives allows the reader to reflect on the impact science has on our daily lives.

Scriptures are used throughout the book to under gird each scientific method and topic presented. This is such a needed book in the culture we currently are living in where people are not able to make the connection between the secular and sacred. Dr. Peete does a wonderful job of making that connection which then allows science and scripture to be accessible to all readers. Dr. Peete's passion for the pursuit of wisdom, knowledge and understanding are evident in each page.

Dr. Robert L. Manaway, Sr.
January 18, 2018

THE BIBLE IS NOT A SCIENCE BOOK BUT…

CHAPTER 1

What is Science?

Science is a way of learning about the natural world through your senses. Science also includes all the knowledge gained from exploring our surrounding environment and beyond.

Our personal definition of science is "human explanation" of God's creative actions resulting in unchangeable universal laws of nature. The Bible stands all test of time and is worthy of investigation through the lens of science.

"Test all things; hold fast what is good." 1 Thessalonian 5:21

The Bible encourages us to study and learn about the world (1 Timothy 2:15). Science is rooted in our efforts to understand and explain the world around us. Our natural inquisitiveness seeks to answers to the 5 W's + H: Who? What? Why? Where? When? and How? Historically, knowledge about our environment came slowly through observations and interpretations of what we perceived through our senses.

Science is a systematic approach of discovering our environment, acquiring knowledge, experiencing new exploits, and answering questions. Science is a tool for problem solving that uses what you already know to find out what you do not know. Our world during ancient biblical times was mainly examined through superstition, astronomy, mythology, ignorance, and religion.

The Bible from Genesis to Revelation is consistent in using descriptors of physical awareness of our world. Science investigations that women and men accomplished in the Bible can be referred as foreknowledge or pre-science inquires. Pre-science is knowledge of things before they existed or happened in a formal or recorded method. Pre-science found in the Bible points to a protective curtain around the Earth that we call the ozone layer; the life cycles of social arthropods in comparison to humans; compositions of lotions, potions and oils from the alchemist; anatomically and physiological structure of the body; the origin of life and the rules of genetics; identification of Stars and their uniqueness in singing and their arrangement in the heaven called constellations; or the effects of invisible life forms called microorganisms.

Modern Science confirms these descriptive phenomena in the Bible. They occurred over periods of time. The Bible is so uniquely design that a verse can tell of a happening that took hundreds even millions of years (Genesis 10:25). Aristotle, an ancient Greek scholar and philosopher proclaimed, "But the whole vital process of the Earth takes place so gradually and in period to time which are so immense compared with the length of our life, which these changes are not observed, and before their course can be recorded from beginning to end, whole nations perish and are destroyed."

The Bible does not directly use the term Science because it was not formalized in the beginning as a discipline until later in the history of civilization.

Introduction: Science Emerges Through the Scriptures

Trust and belief in the Scriptures is hinged and anchored on Faith. It is fuel by hope and invisible substances that is revealed through the evidence that is all around us (Hebrew 11:1-2). The main goal of the Bible is to show the salvific relationship between God and humankind; from their creation, their fall, and their eventual rise. The Bible serves as an instructional guide book (**B**asic-**I**nstruction-**B**efore-**L**eaving-**E**arth) for living.

The main goal of Science is to explain and provide basic understanding and coping skills for life. This is accomplished when using observable, measurable, repeatable evidence that describe and explain our environment: the sky, ocean, the land and ourselves. Science helps to explain the how's, what's, when's, and where's of the interdependence and interactions of biotic (living) and (abiotic)non-living parts of the universe. Only God knows the why's. Why does grass contain a green pigment or brown for soil, purple mountains, blue skies, and red for blood?

Scaffolding, progressing towards stronger understanding, can bring together Science and Faith. It is possible to be believe of Science with a Strong Faith in God, Elohim (the creator). Christians can embrace science with open arms and minds because God made science. "For in God all things were created: things in heaven and on Earth, visible and invisible, whether thrones or powers or rulers or authorities; all things have been created through God and for God" Colossians 1:16. When we study science, it opens opportunities to experience the serenity, glory, and majesty of God. This will lead to deeper and more meaningful worship. "Worship the Lord in the splendor of His holiness. Tremble before him, all the Earth! The world is firmly established; it cannot be moved. Let the heavens rejoice, let the Earth be glad; let them say among the nations, "The Lord reigns!" Let the sea resound, and all that is in it; let the fields be jubilant, and everything in them! Let the trees of the forest sing, let them sing for joy before the Lord" 1 Chronicles 16:29-33.

The Bible is not a book the describes cellular activities. Nor is it a physics book that expounds on the electrical interactions of electrons, protons, and neutrons. Neither is it an Earth Science book that describes the tectonic shifting of the Earth's crust that cause quaking and shaking. Lastly it is not a medical book of surgical techniques and technologies. However, consider the following before drawing any final conclusions." Prove all things; hold fast what which is good"1 Thessalonian 5:21

Think on these things. The Bible is:

- not **a biology** book but it gives us insight into the origin and purpose of all life and that blood is the river of life- Genesis 1, Leviticus 17:11

- not a **botany** book but it gives us insight on the complete life cycle of a plant through overnight germination to production of fruit from a single dry almond branch-Numbers 17:8-9

- not a **physics** book but it gives us insight into energy transformation- Law of conservation of Energy:" We shall be changed. Changed from mortal to immortality in a twinkling of an eye"- 1 1Corinthians 15:51-52

- not an **astronomy** book but it gives us insight into the purpose of our Sun, Moon, Stars, and Planets – Genesis 1:14-19

- not a **geology** book but it gives us insight when the large land masses (Pangaea) separated into continents and islands – Genesis 10:25

- not an **oceanography** book but it gives us insight that there are paths flowing through the sea- Psalm 8:8

- not a **history** book but it gives us insight of the beginning of civilization with Cain in the land of Nod – Genesis 4:16-17

- not a **biomedical technology** manual but it gives us insight into the beginning steps to surgery and the extraction of adult stems cells from the marrow of rib bone – Genesis 2:21-23

- not an **etymology** book but it gives us insight of the origin of world languages at the tower of Babel -Genesis 11:6-8

- not a **social and political science** book but it gives us insight in the rise and fall of families and nations – Jeremiah 46

- not a **genetic** book but it gives us insight about chromosomes and the importance of following the rule "reproduction after your own kind"- Genesis 2:18

- not a **chemistry** book of formulas but it gives us insight for making holy oil, perfumes for spa baths for Queen Esther, the gigantic spice-rack transported by Queen of Sheba to King Solomon in search of wisdom - 1 Kings 10; 2 Chronicles 9
- not a **Periodic table of natural elements** but gives us insight into use of elements like Gold, Silver, Iron, and Tin probably used by the first metal smith – Genesis 4:22
- not a manual on **animal preservation or reservation** but it gives us insight about a man named Noah that saved a portion of humanity and build a floating animal sanctuary –Genesis 7:2
- not **a geochemical book** of cycles but it gives us insight how water molecules transpire, evaporate, and condense into clouds and fall as precipitation- Isaiah 55:10
- not an **anatomy and physiology** book but gives us insight into the order of formation and arrangement of scattered bones into a skeletal frame with joints, organs, muscles, tendons and ligaments, skin, and breath in shaping the human body –Ezekiel 37:1-14
- not a book exploring the **properties and principles of light** but gives us insight of the behavior of reflecting and refracting light waves when the Sun's radiant beams hit rain drops and create a phenomenon in the sky called a rainbow –Genesis 9:13
- not a book for **cardiac-respiratory** specialist but gives us insight how Adam became an animated clay man after God puffed His breath into his body and initiated aerobic respiration- Genesis 2:7
- not a book of **textiles** but gives insight about the possible beginning of fire proofed or insulated clothing- Daniel 3:21-27
- not a book of **aerodynamics** but give us insight into what damages a small projectile (a smooth stone) with the right acceleration can do to a giant's head-1 Samuel 17:4-51

- 📖 not a book about molecular **attraction** but gives us insight of the attractive cohesive and buoyant forces of water as Peter and Jesus walked on water –

- 📖 not a book of **archeology** that theorized a seven-feet wide asteroid millions of years ago was hurling through space at the speed of more than 40,000 miles per hour towards Earth. On impact caused an explosion that released the energy equivalent to billions of atomic bombs that killed all the dinosaurs, but gives us insight of the story of Lucifer/Satan hurling through space like lightning and crashing on Earth. Luke 10:18; Ezekiel 28; Isaiah 14

- 📖 not a book of **cytology**-the study of cells that proclaims the foundation theory that all living things come from pre-existence cells but gives us insight that Eve, the first woman, was created from the pre-existing cells originating from red marrow in Adam's, the first man, ribs.-Genesis2:22

- 📖 not a book of **acoustics** that describe molecules in solids that can be set to vibrating, or changing their frequency and pitch but gives us insight how a wall in the town of Jericho came tumbling down after soldiers marching in circles , in silence became radically noisy , shouting soldiers –Joshua 6

- 📖 The Bible is a book of **truths** with minimal explanations or details but foundational little chunks of information. "The secret things belong to the Lord our God but those things which are revealed belong to us and to our children forever" Deuteronomy 29:2

An example of early science is mentioned in the Bible is found in the book of Prophet Daniel. Daniel and his young companions were in captivity in Babylon. They were selected as children with no blemish, well favored to be educated in special school to be skillful in all wisdom, cunning in knowledge, and understanding science (Daniel 1:3-4). Science began in Egypt and Babylon with mathematics, metallurgy, anatomy, and astronomy. Daniel was most likely trained in all sciences.

The Bible does discuss the importance of gathering knowledge, pursuing wisdom, and learning about things. "The secret things belong to the Lord our God; but those things which are revealed belong to us and to our children forever, that we may do all the words of this law" (Deuteronomy 29:29). God told Moses that he called Bazaleel and filled him with the Spirit of God in wisdom, understanding, knowledge, and all manner of craftmanship. Bazaleel was also given an assistance called Aholiab who was full of wisdom (Exodus 31: 1-6). God did give these men and workers a type of science. The book of Ecclesiastes reveals Solomon reasonings, searching, and findings as he was in quest to satisfy his dissatisfaction. However, he discovered the following truths with scientific bases: The Earth is eternal; Sun circuits; wind circuits; season and times for all things; creation was made perfect; water circuit; both humankind and animals die physically and go back to the dust; and two are better than one. (Ecclesiastes 1;4)

Reflectively, through observations, asking questions, and exploration lead to the primary approaches in which I was introduced to Scriptures and informal science lessons in the home. My natural curiosity was the open door to faith and science. Home can provide an atmosphere to be able to ask questions that will reveal that you are thinking about your environment. "Start children off on the way they should go, and even when they are old they will not turn from it " (Proverbs 22:6).

DISCOVERY SCIENCE

CHAPTER 2

The scientific method evolved over time. Aristotle is given partial credit along with other Greek philosophers in the western civilization.
Aristotle was the founder of an empirical science based on experimentation or observation. During the golden age, between the 10th and 14th centuries, an Islam Muslim scholar developed a scientific process.

They were the first to use experiments and observation as the basis of science. Many historians regard science as starting during this period. Al-Haytham, the scholar, is accredited as the architect of the scientific method. Al-Haytham was an Arab, Muslim scientist, astronomer, mathematician, and philosopher. In Europe, he was nick-named "Ptolemy the Second" or "The Physicist". His scientific method involved the following modern-day steps:

- Asking a question/Problem
- Research-finding out what you can about the topic
- Hypothesis-an educated guess
- Testing your hypothesis /Experiment
- Collecting Data and doing Analysis
- Drawing Conclusions

Many valuable lessons that help to frame our lives are learned from our own homes/community and through diverse faith tradition. Home is a sacred meeting place where you might acquire a strong foundation, benefit from wisdom stories, receive instructions, develop critical thinking skills, and acquire knowledge and strategies needed for success in life.

Generally, in ancient times Hebrew fathers or grandfathers were the formal heads of the household and his word was law. Hebrew mothers and girls were vessels of wisdom and local history. Women married into new families and had varied expertise and experiences within diverse settings other than their native tribe or village.

Many women worked out of their home; like Lydia and the Proverbs 32 woman, in trade and merchandising. They invented, crafted, and developed new processes, and technologies needed for survival in the wilderness, deserts, and foreign lands. The early Hebrew were nomadic tent dwellers and use the resources of whatever materials they found. They were early scientists. Observing their environment and perhaps asking many questions and seeking answers.

Biblical Women were STEM skilled and knew how to:

- Construct tents made of dark brown or black goatskins and camel hairs with strips of leather sewn together to make a waterproof surface. These strips were stretched over a wooden frame and held secured with cords pegged. Women mainly put up the tents and fetched the water for settlement.

- Searched out grazing pastures for the animals to eat and drink

- Excavate pits in the ground for storing grains

- Cook over hearth and oven craved out of holes in the ground.

- Recycling dung to be used as organic fuel

- Perform circumcisions and delivered baby with the skillfulness of physicians or surgeon hands

- Grind grains into flour, pressing and fermenting grapes into wine

- Salt fish to slow down decay

- Using members of the Fungi species, like yeast, that increases dough volume

- Treatment for illness caused by microorganisms - invisible bacteria and viruses
- Lift water from deep well with early simple machines like pulley systems

One of the oldest methods of how women and girls figured out new ideas and concepts on their own was by trial and error, local superstitions, listening, observing, and just being a little curious. These learning modes refined ideas and new understanding that lead to new knowledge, understandings, application and synthesis of information.

The Scriptures admonish and encourage mature women to train the younger women and girls and share their insight. "One generation shall commit your works to another, and shall declare your mighty acts" (Psalm 145:4).

My entrance into the world of science was formalized through wisdom, cooking, faith lessons from my Grandmother Sarah. Grandmother Sarah Handshaw-Butts was a huge inspiration to me that had a profound impact on my life and love of science. My Grandma Sarah was a lady of eloquence, quiet nature but firm, a good listener with a sweet smile, and strong faith in God.

In the middle of my elementary years my father became very ill and was not able to work for a long period. This placed great financial stress on the welfare of my family.

My mother's parents, Bishop Robert C. Butts and Sarah Handshaw Butts, came to our rescue and invited us to come and stay in their new home in West Baltimore. They were the second or third African American family to integrate that neighborhood in the early fifties. It was a lovely five-bedroom home that set on a hill with a white wraparound porch and double French doors on the side of the house that open to the garden and backyard, filled with several fruit trees and bunny rabbits. When I stepped into the foyer I was welcome with the sparkling light from an overhead crystal chandelier. I was ready for something new and exciting. This home is where my science adventure or exploits with Grandma began. Words fail to capture my love for her. She impressed upon me that faith and trust in God, determination, a good education, and hard work would bring me success. Her favorite verse or most quoted verse bestowed as a blessing on my life were, "Trust in the LORD with all your heart and lean not unto your own understanding. In all your ways acknowledge him, and he shall direct your paths" (Proverbs 3:5-6).

My grandparents' home was filled with resources that included many reading materials. My siblings and I had close at hand the latest sets of *Encyclopedia Britannica*, dictionaries, magazines, newspapers, radio, and television. Our detached garage was filled with different types of tools, gadgets and gizmos. It was a great place of exploration and discovery. There were many places around the house where you could create, investigate, read quietly, and meditate for a while. I took advantage of every opportunity to steal away in a quiet corner in a big comfortable chair in front of a picture window in the living room and just think.

I was quite a curious and inquisitive little girl, always asking the questions 'why this or why that'. Grandma provided many occasions for conversations between us. She would attentively listen to me and often answer my barrage of questions with the statement, "Why are we sending you to school? Think girl! Think!" And I did 'think' about it. Education was very important to Grandma, and her desires were for my siblings and myself to do well and make the family and community proud.

Many of the things that I needed to know about early science was shown to me on the first floor of Grandma Sarah's home in the kitchen. Just as the Bible recorded the events foundations of pre- science during ancient time, working with my grandmother provided deposits of learning for me. Grandma told me it was okay to tell everyone what we did together --- and I did. And these are a few things I learned.

All substances are made of matter. The matter is anything that occupies space and has mass. Matter can be solids, liquids, or gasses. Both recipes and science experiments consist of forms of matter to measure and instructions to follow.

Physical and chemical reactions in the lab and kitchen will vary and encourage you to find a solution to reactions that caused things to change colors, or phases or even dissolve (disappear)and combine to form new substances from the effects of increase or decrease temperature that might lead to shrinking or expansion, swelling, vaporization, melting, burning, and precipitation (bubbles). For example, when we place water on the flame of the gas burner soon it would increase temperature, get warmer to hot and soon disappear or evaporate into a little cloud called steam.

The Chemistry of Baking a Cake with Grandma Sarah

Under the kitchen table was a large, ten-gallon metal' air-tight container. It was filled with all the wonderful things that could be turned into a delicious yellow cake with chocolate frosting: the flour, baking soda, chocolate powder, baking powder, powdered sugar, granulated white sugar, and sometimes cornmeal was all kept in this metal can. If Grandma Sarah needed something out of the container, she always insisted that the lid was put back on immediately and checked that it was replaced with a tight fit.

I often wondered why she kept those items in the tin can. She answered my inquiries that the flour and some of the other ingredients needed to be kept dry and safe from little critters and bugs. The containers also keep everything cool in the humid summer weather of Baltimore, Maryland.

Now, the time has come for Grandma to bake one of her wonderful yellow cakes with chocolate icing. Ummm- yummy good. Her basic recipe consisted of the following: softened butter, sugar, eggs, all-purpose flour, baking soda and baking powder, milk, vanilla extract, and salt.

Of course, I wanted to help Grandma prepare the cake batter but most importantly if I watched, assisted, and waited patiently I could get the opportunity to lick the spoon. Often there would be a battle if my siblings were around about who would get the honor to lick the spoon covered with delicious batter fresh out the bowl. At that time, we did not have the fear of bacterium *Salmonellas Enteritidis* in raw eggs that can cause vomiting and diarrhea. Scientists say today we can start to lick the spoon again because of the improved health of eggs on the market.

We started our cooking adventure with two large bowls, large wooden spoons with long handles, sifter, measuring cups, measuring spoons and turning on the oven to 350 degrees, and collecting all the ingredients.

Each ingredient has a job to do. Flour provides the structure; baking powder and baking soda give the cake its airiness; eggs bind the ingredients; butter and oil tenderize; sugar sweetens, and milk or water provides moisture.

First, we put on our aprons or she would have wrapped my waist in a big towel around my waist. And next, we shifted the flour. That was fun but why do it fly in the air and your clothes get covered with some flour. Grandma said the sifting would make the cake lighter.

Sifting is meant to aerate the flour before it is incorporated into a dough or batter. A lot of time the flour has been sitting in the cupboard packed or compressed in bags. The process of sifting helps to remove large lumps in the flour. Also, if you sift the flour with other ingredients such as leavening agents or salt, it helps disperse those ingredients into one mixture before adding them to liquid ingredients.

In two clean bowls, we mixed the wet ingredients in one and in the other we mixed the dry ingredients. We had to get all the ingredient in the right order and right amount. We put baking powder and baking soda in the flour to help it to pop and rise. Grandma told me if we put too much baking soda or baking powder in the flour the cake might not taste very good. It might also have a little metallic taste. Creamy butter was added to help keep the cake moist and reduce going stale.

Combing the dry and wet ingredients put them to work – the protein in the flour bond and create gluten, giving the cake its flexibility. Eggs hold the mixture together. Baking powder and baking soda each release carbon dioxide, adding bubbles to the butter, helping it expand. A cake batter that flows means that the hydration is consistent.

Grandma warned me when I begged her to help in mixing the batter not to over mix the batter.
If you keep mixing it might become too runny or lumpy.
Gluten is a general name for the proteins found in wheat. Gluten helps foods maintain their shape, acting as the glue that holds food together. When gluten aligns, the proteins align with strands.

If the batter is too runny, you have disrupted the network that are formed.

Grandma took over beating the cake mixture. She beat the cake batter until it was silky and smooth, then poured it into the prepared greased and floured cake pans. The cake pans were next placed in the hot oven.

The ingredients change again when the batter is in the oven. The starch portion of the flour gels – with help from sugar - and creates a web-like structure that traps water and provides moisture. The carbon dioxide from the baking powder or baking soda will expand the cake. Gluten holds those bubbles in place while the fat from the oil or butter lubricates the process.

I was anxious to get the cakes out of the oven. I wanted to open the oven door to check on the progress of the cakes. I was cautioned not to do this because I could get burned and the cakes might fall.

Do not take the cake out early. It can collapse because the structure has not set yet.

The cakes were baked for about one hour, then removed from the oven, and left to cool on the counter.

Sugar and fat also play a role when a cake cools. Sugar helps slow the cake from hardening. When a cake begins to go stale, the starch starts to crystallize. Sugar will draw the water and prevent the starch molecules from forming and crystallizing.

Now, it was time to make the chocolate icing. The chunk of chocolate was heated over a special pan she called a double boiler until the chocolate was melted, smooth, and glossy. She added some other items to make the chocolate soft but fluffy. Next, she covered the top and side of the cake with icing using a spatula. The cake was put in a cake container and on display.

Grandma always put a small test cake pan in the oven, so we could get a sample before the grand cake was cut. Oh, so delicious! I experienced so much fun learning how to cook with Grandma Sarah.

Recipes are like science experiments. In a science experiment, you begin with a question and an educated guess, sometimes charts or diagrams are included. Then your experiment will give you information on things you must measure. Next, the procedure is the steps you take to follow through your experiment and keeping notes, data on the results in your conclusion. If it seems like your hypothesis fail start over with a new question and design a new experiment. Our senses help us to be more aware of our environment. We use our senses for touching, tasting, seeing, hearing, and feeling. Learning becomes meaningful and memorable when activities involve the use of all the senses.

A recipe is a set of instructions preparing a dish. It includes a list of the description of the food, ingredients required, amounts needed, and the way they are to be combined, and a picture or photo. The recipe also names or tell you what you will be making. You can also consider recipe synonymous to formula or blueprint. By following directions, step-by-step helps to generate new idea and curiosities that lead to better skills in math, reading, science, communication and culture, as well as, building good memories.

Baking is a great way to discover science. The scientist and Grandma Sarah both share somethings in common. They each had a special place to carry out their work. Grandma used her kitchen and a scientist has a laboratory.

A scientist's experiment consists of a series of steps or instructions. A recipe is similar to the scientific method or process in that you must be precise in measurements, combing ingredients that might react explosively with each other, and following established processes. The scientific method is an organized method of doing things. The scientific method is used when you cook or bake through things that use heat, water, acids (vinegar), bases (baking soda), adding air to mixtures by whipping, mixing oils to change the state of things, and using salt to preserve.

In recipes and scientific instruction use action verbs. A verb are words for describing actions, states, or occurrences. Active verbs like stir, pour, separate, chop, peel, heat, whip or freeze can be found in recipes. Active verbs like examine, compare, collect, dissect, cut, measure, weight, increase, observe, and mix can be found in procedure for an experiment.

Another way that science and baking are similar is they both must read through the process to follow, next they must collect all the ingredients and equipment they will use.

Vanilla Cupcake Recipe	Scientific method in Reading a Recipe
Preheat the oven to 350 and line a 12-cup muffin pan with paper liners **Prepare** your batter **Whisk** 1/3 cup flour, 1 teaspoon salt in a bowl **Beat** 1 stick softened butter in a separate bowl with a mixer on medium-high speed until smooth for 1 minute **Add** 1 cup sugar and beat until creamy, for 4 minutes **Beat** in 2 eggs, one at a time 2 teaspoons vanilla **Beat** in the flour mixture in three batches on low speed, alternating with 1.2 cup of milk total **Beat** on medium high speed until just combined **Divided** the batter among the muffin cups. **Bake** until the tops spring back, 20 to 25 minutes **Transfer** to a rack and let cool 5 minutes in the pan **Remove** the cupcakes to the rack to cool completely **Make** your frosting, then **pipe or spread** on the cupcakes	**State the Problem**: How can you determine if a detergent that contains enzymes, called proteases, can clean clothing? **Form** a hypothesis that explains how a protein mixture might affect stained removal by a detergent that contains a protease (enzymes). **Put on** a lab apron, safety goggles, and gloves **Use** tongs or a hot mitt to handle heated glassware **Put** 18 g or regular gelatin in a 150-ml beaker. **Slowly add** 50 ml of boiling water to the beaker and stir the mixture with a glass stirring rod **Test and record** the pH of this solution **Very slowly** add 0.1 g of $NaHCHO_3$, (baking soda) to the hot gelatin while stirring Note any reactions. **Test and record** the pH of the solution **Place** six test tubes in a test-tube rack **Pour** 5 ml of the gelatin-$NaHCHO_3$ mixture into each tube **Cover** the tubes and store them at room temperature until you are ready to test stained fabric samples **Design** an experiment to test your hypothesis

Grandma's recipes were originally handed down from past generations. We had tasted the dish before and enjoyed it. The proof of it goodness was in the tasting. We trusted the ingredients and believe that following instructions we would get a great dish just like our ancestors. The Bible also contains guides and trusted instructions handed down from generation to generation like a cookbook. Reading a cookbook will not guarantee you the honor of becoming a chef. The difference is you must do more than only read. The cookbook or the Bible. You must apply that you read and believed. The Bible is like a recipe for life on how to be a follower of Christ, "Oh taste and see that God's word is good" (Psalm 34:*8*) .

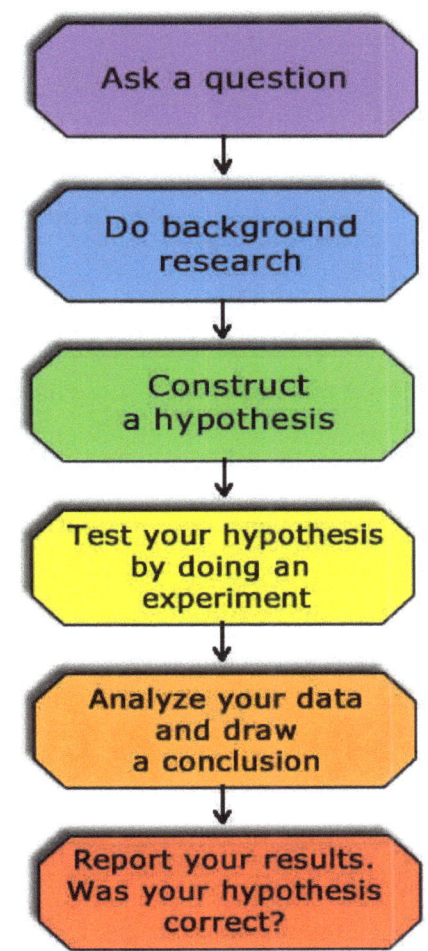

Grandma's Hands
Bessie Lockett-Peete

My father's mother, Grandma Peete, was another great cook and gardener in the family. Through her experience, wisdom, and knowledge in the kitchen, she also provided more opportunities to spark my inquisitiveness and open the doors to exploring science in action.

The family frequently visited my Grandma Peete a few times throughout the year to what we called 'going to the country. She resided in a home built by my grandfather in the small town of Franklin, Virginia.

During some of the visits, we shared several mornings and afternoons in the kitchen. One of the lessons I vibrantly remember occurred the first time I stayed, on my own, for a few weeks and watched her cook on the big, black, wood stove in the kitchen.

This was the first time I saw anyone cook on the wood stove. I was amazed and wanted to know how it worked. That big black stove was both phenomenal and scary at the same time to me. I was accustomed to seeing food cooked on a four-burner white enamel gas stove in a garden view kitchen. However, I was very curious and ready for an adventure.

The wood stove served many purposes in the home. Grandma Peete also used the stove for heating the flat iron and drying clothes. The flat iron was made of heavy metal and had to be gripped with a pad or thick rag. Granddaddy Peete was an Elder in the church, and it was essential to always look his best. She had two irons on the stove when pressing granddad's white starched shirts and suit pants. One was in use and the other one for reheating.

She would iron fabric without the benefit of electricity and put an almost permanent straight crease in his pants. Experience and probably trial and error told her when the iron was hot enough but not so hot that it would scorch the fabric.

Heat is transferred by conduction, convection, and radiation. Heat travels through solid by conduction. Conduction means the transfer of energy from one molecule to the next molecule. Most metals are good conductors of heat, while wood is a poor conductor. That is why the flat iron and frying pans are made of metal and often have wooden handles.

I also saw her test the flat iron temperature by sprinkling water off her hands onto the flat side of the iron. The iron would make a loud hissing sound. The water on the iron's surface would create steam, indicating the surface wore hot and ready to be used. The clothes to be ironed were also sprinkled with water. This would help to create steam. Steam aided in removing the wrinkles from the clothing.

Another use of the wood stove was heating water for baths and heating the circulating cold air for that section of the house. I was never allowed to cook on the stove, but I could collect logs or wood that my Granddaddy Peete had chopped for the stove. He would build a woodpile in the back yard placed in several rows of logs creating a tower in sometimes placed in a shaped form that resembled a triangle.

Firewood just dumped in a heap will not dry, and it will not burn well. Rain will run down and soak into cut ends while ground moisture will migrate up and soak into the spongy inner bark.

The main cooking was done on a wood-burning stove in the kitchen. My grandmother could make the best biscuits anyone had ever tasted. They were big, thick, bumpy, but very fluffy and delicious. When they were lightly brown on top she would pull them out of the oven and serve them with a little butter, Brer Rabbit molasses, and thick slices of bacon. To this day, if I see a bottle of Brer Rabbit molasses, I think about my Grandma and those hot biscuits.

Science behind a Wood stove-Thermodynamics

Wood is developed by the process called photosynthesis. This process involved water, carbon dioxide, sunlight (radiant energy), and minerals from the soil. The light energy of the sun will be converted to chemical energy in the wood.

Grandma would select her wood carefully. She would classify the wood as too green, or too dry or too wet. When I was asked to get wood for the cooking I was directed to get the wood from certain piles.

Greenwood contains high contents of moisture/water. Before the wood can burn, the water must be out of the wood. Greenwood is split and left to season for a year or two before burning it. This allowed the sun to dry the wood. The radiant energy would help wick away the moisture from greenwood.

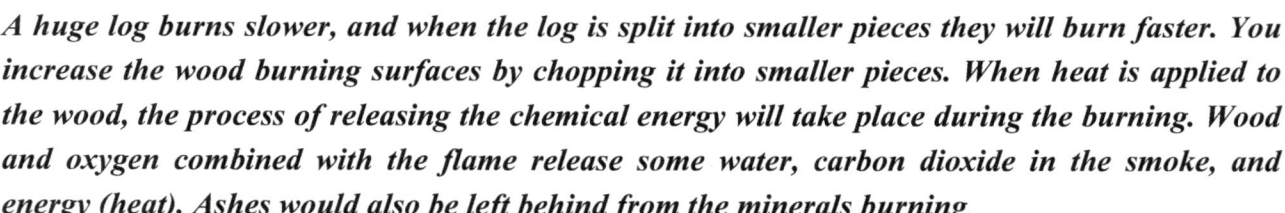

Grandma told me that dry wood burns faster, and green wood burned slower. Some of the other wood that was selected were splintered sticks, quarter-cut logs, and other were huge block or chunks.

A huge log burns slower, and when the log is split into smaller pieces they will burn faster. You increase the wood burning surfaces by chopping it into smaller pieces. When heat is applied to the wood, the process of releasing the chemical energy will take place during the burning. Wood and oxygen combined with the flame release some water, carbon dioxide in the smoke, and energy (heat). Ashes would also be left behind from the minerals burning.

I watched her take small sticks of wood and some rolled up pieces of paper and ignite them with a match. The match would supply enough heat energy to get the wood burning.

"Fire-lighting, however simple is an operation requiring some skill; a fire is readily made by laying a few cinders at the bottom in open order; over this a few pieces of paper, and over that again eight or ten pieces of dry wood; over the wood, a course of moderate-sized pieces of coal, taking care to leave hollow spaces between for air at the center; and taking care to lay the whole

well back in the grate, so that the smoke may go up the chimney, and not into the room. This done, fire the paper with a match from below, and, if properly laid, it will soon burn up; the stream of flame from the wood and paper soon communicating to the coals and cinders, provided there is plenty of air at the center". (*Isabella Beeton,* Book of Household Management, *1861*)

At times the stove would be roaring with heat and the room was toasty and warm or extremely hot. To speed up the burning process, she would add some more wood or increase the amount of air (oxygen).

The damper on the stove pipe would be open or closed to control the amount of air that comes into the stove. If the damper was closed, the fire slowed down. If the damper was open, the fire would increase.

The fire never went completely out in the stove. In the evening before going to bed, I watched Granddaddy Peete arrange logs or huge chunks of wood and pieces of wood to be sure a small fire was available in the morning. Similarly, I noticed that all the other homes we would visit also had black wood stoves.
If the surface is black, it will radiate heat well. A light-colored stove will not radiate as well.

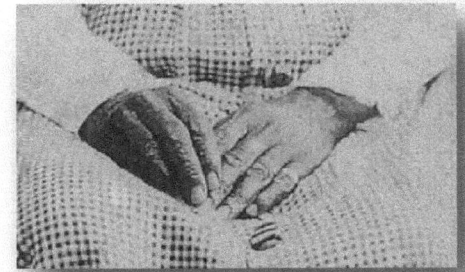

Grandma's Peete Loving Hands- muscles, tendons, and ligaments

Her hands were big, bold, smooth skin, dark in pigment, yet gentle and loving. She would squeeze, press, and roll with her hands the dough. This was a type of massaging or kneading. Bending the wrist and or moving her fingers brings muscles and tendons into actions. I called it the fingers dance that encouraged the shortening when pressed into flakes to fully cooperate.

The fingers of your hand have a row of three bones called phalanges, running down the center and each thumb has two phalanges. Your fingers bend at the knuckle joints, where the phalanges are held together by ligaments, muscles, and tendons. Ligaments are places where muscles are attached to muscles and tendons are the places where muscles are attached to bones.

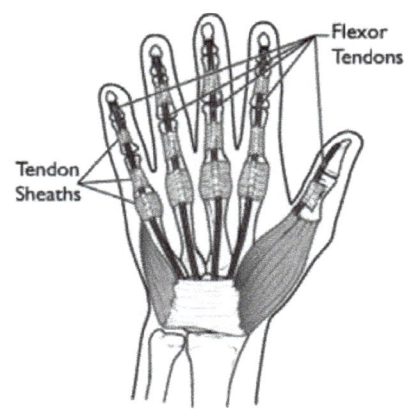

The finger joints are lined with cartilage. When cartilage is compressed by the motion of a finger, a very slippery fluid, called synovial fluid, oozes out to lubricate the joint. Synovial fluid reduces the friction to almost nothing. This helps reduce wear and tear on joint surfaces as two adjacent phalanges slide against each other. The major muscles that power your fingers are in your forearm. There are also smaller muscles located in your hands. The muscles you use when straightening your hand out of a fist are called extensors and are located on top of the lower arm.

It was important to pay attention to your sense of touch when working the dough. Grandma said you knead the dough until it feels light. If you overhandled the dough it will feel heavy and dense.

Our hands are covered with tactile sensors. These sensors can detect pressure, temperature, pain, touch.

Let's Cook Biscuits

Some adults and kids today only know that biscuits come out of a can or tube that goes "whop" when you beat it on the side of the table or counter top. Grandma Peete did not have a written recipe. She cooked numerous times for eight children, a husband, friends, and the church. She turned out the tastiest treats from her oven: pies, rolls, savory dishes, and fried chicken. I still remember watching her rhythmic strong hands working the dough. Simple ingredients of flour, baking powder, salt, lard, and cold buttermilk was the short list of things needed for the tasty biscuits.

Mounds of flour with a well or depression in the center was on the kitchen table as a dash of baking powder and a pinch of salt were mixed into the flour. Scoops of lard was integrated into the flour. I watch in amazement as her hand twisting and fingers moved to transform the flour and lard into little marbles.

Patiently she worked all the simple ingredients together in a satin-tight ball dusted with flour. Then she would begin to pull off dough balls, roll it in the palm of her hands covered with flour. Gently but keeping the rhythm by humming old hymns, she tossed the dough from hand to hand. Shaping and molding the biscuit. One final pat and the biscuits were placed on a greased cooking sheet. Sometimes I could participate by using inverted wide-mouth jelly jars to cut the biscuits out of the flour.

Making biscuits is both an art and science. But the science behind the ingredients is quite interesting. First, let's examine why Grandma always used lard and no other fats, like butter or other shortenings.

Lard (fats) is the fat of pig located around the kidneys. Buttermilk is added to the flour-lard mixture. Buttermilk will improve the flavor, texture, and color. It is made from the fermentation of milk with lactic-acid producing bacteria. This gives buttermilk its tangy flavor, which adds complexity and depth to the finished baked goods. Buttermilk also slows microbial growth.

I helped by getting the buttermilk which was kept in the ice box. Before refrigeration, foods were kept cool in the ice box. The ice box was cooled by a huge block of ice inside. My Grandfather sold blocks of ice. Going to visit my father's parents was an entirely new world of astonishment for a city kid. When I opened the door to the ice box all the food was around or near the ice and to my surprise it was very cold inside. The thick walls of the ice box, served as insulation. I was told to be sure I closed the door to the ice box immediately and shut tightly.

The baking powder had been added to the flour. Baking powder served as a leavening and went to work as soon as the dough gets wet and start forming invisible bubbles in which you can only see the evidence of the gas in the rise of the dough.

This powder is an alkaline that when it encounters an acidic ingredient (buttermilk) produces carbon dioxide and lifts the dough.

Science is everywhere and there is no permanent descriptor of who is a scientist and what a scientist looks like. I learned and experienced early science with my grandparents and my parents through touching, tasting, seeing, smelling, feeling, and listening. All were needed for spontaneous or nonintrusive inquiries into my environment. Cooking activities were ideal for me because all my senses and curiosities were stimulated while I was learning life lessons and having fun. As a child, I took these times as normal for being with my grandmother.

When a person's senses are engaged as they are during cooking experiences, learning becomes meaningful and memorable.

SEARCHING THE SCRIPTURES

CHAPTER 3

The Bible is sacred and holy. It is a collection of 66 books written by different authors over a span of many years. The Bible is divided into two divisions that consist of the Old Testament (39 books) and the New Testament (27 books). The Bible records the interactions of God with historical people and nations. The Bible reveals the meaning of life and the responsibility of humans to God. The Bible is instructive, the world's best seller, and the world's most translated book.

Faith comes by hearing. Science comes by seeing What did they see?

The first three words that open the first book of the Bible, Genesis, are "In the beginning." Everything has a beginning and an ending.
Green plant life cycle begins with a seed. Multicellular animal life begins with the union of an egg and sperm.

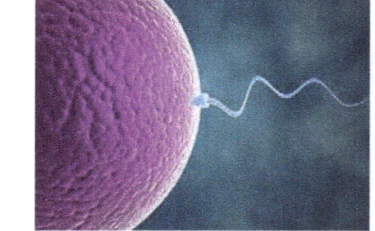

Starting with the book of Genesis our emphasis is on the natural world of plants, animals, people, galaxies, atoms, and forces. This is the beginning of the foundation for science evolving within the contents of Bible stories. Science is a body of knowledge, processes, and discoveries. Genesis reveals how this discipline was first practiced by two humans called Adam and Eve in a pristine world. This couple was on a journey of informal lifelong learning. Lifelong learning is the "ongoing, voluntary, and self-motivated" pursuit of knowledge. Learning which enabled them to gain new information and apply it to solving problems or coping with changes. The knowledge they obtained improved or enhanced their self- sustainability, advanced communication between them, promoted citizenship as cities grew, development of technology to upgrade or invent better tools and broaden understanding of the stresses of family and everyday life.

Apostle Paul wrote in second Timothy 3:16-17, "All Scripture is inspired by God and profitable for teaching, for reproof, for correction, for training in righteousness; that the people of God may be adequate, equipped for every good work." Moses inscribed in Deuteronomy 29:29, "The secret things belong to the Lord our God, but those things which are revealed belong to us and to our children forever, that we may do all the words of this law. "The Bible is a treasured book of faith, not a scientific textbook that contains questions, facts, hypotheses, laws, and theories. Faith is not science. The dictionary defines faith as having confidence or trust in a person or thing. The Bible states that faith is simply believing something that we do not actually concretely "see."(Hebrews 11:1). The Bible as a book of faith centers on complete trust and confidence in a sovereign God. This belief system does not rest on logical proof or material evidence that speaks about basic scientific principles in everyday language and experiences.

Throughout the Bible, you will uncover observations, superstitions, curiosities, and interaction with the physical and biological natural environment. Nonliving and living elements are found in lessons laced with life instructions through parables, metaphors, symbols, and similes as well as allegories. A parable uses illustrations that make a comparison with things that are familiar, instructions or truths to teach not offend, and principles with the purpose to govern our lives, "I will open my mouth in parables; I will utter what has been hidden since the foundation of the world." (Matthew 13:35).

You will find in the Bible figurative language that relates or uses what things are **like** rather than what they are. Two kinds of figurative language regularly used are similes and metaphors. A metaphor is a figure of speech based on implied comparisons. A metaphor says 'something is something else.' A simile is a comparison between two, unlike things. A simile says 'something is like something else.' The word **like** or **as** usually appears in similes.

Some examples of figurative language found in Scripture that uses nature as basic science prompts:

- "Behold, I send you out as sheep in the midst of wolves. Therefore, be wise as serpents and harmless as doves" (Matthew 10:16).
- "For they came up with their cattle and their tents, and they came like swarms of locusts" (Judges 6:5).
- "His countenance was like lightning, and his clothing as white as snow" (Matthew 28:3).
- "A word fitly spoken is like apples of gold in pictures of silver" (Proverbs 25:11).
- "Listen! A farmer went out to sow his seed. As he was scattering the seed, some fell along the path, and the birds came and ate it up. Some fell on rocky places, where it did not have much soil. It sprang up quickly because the soil was shallow. But when the sun came up, the plants were scorched, and they withered because they had no root. Other seeds fell among thorns, which grew up and choked the plants so that they did not bear grain. Still, other seed fell on good soil. It came up, grew and produced a crop, some multiplying thirty, some sixty, some a hundred times." Then Jesus said, "Whoever has ears to hear, let them hear." (Mark 4:3-9).
- - "He said to the crowd: "When you see a cloud rising in the west, immediately you say, 'It's going to rain,' and it does. And when the south wind blows, you say, 'It's going to be hot,' and it is. Hypocrites! You know how to interpret the appearance of the Earth and

the sky. How is it that you don't know how to interpret this present time?" (Luke 12:54-56).

☐ "As the rain and the snow come down from heaven, and do not return to it without watering the earth and making it bud and flourish so that it yields seed for the sower and bread to the eater." That is, the rain and snow do not return in this form. The moisture returns and then falls again as rain and snow" (Isaiah 55:10 Psalm 135:7; Jeremiah 10:13).

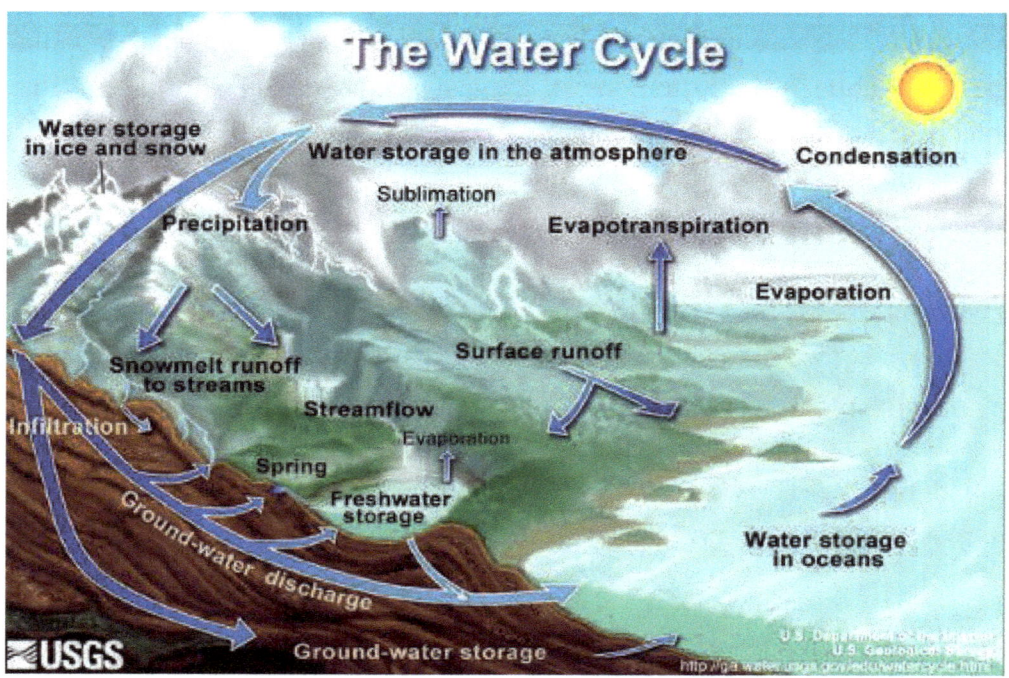

> "Genesis and modern science are answering different questions. Genesis explains who God is and how He relates to the created world. Science elucidates the God-given laws that explain natural phenomena; and form these laws scientists can work backwards to trace the course of the universe's development. Science makes us aware of the infinite power and wisdom of the Creator, but it cannot explain God's purpose in creating universe, or his character. Genesis is not dealing with the issues raised by twentieth century science but with ideas current in the ancient orient over 3,000 year ago."
>
> *The New Bible Commentary/edited by D. Guthrie, J.A. Motyer. 1970: p61*

Science and religion do not have to conflict with each other. Science cannot support or contradict the existence of God. Accepting information about your world by asking questions and seeking answers does not require you giving up your religious faith or belief system. Science is a way of knowing, thinking, and comparing inorganic materials versus organic materials, biotic components in competition with abiotic components of the physical and invisible world that surrounds us.

Science helps us understand and shape our daily lives. It helps us as we interact with our environment.

Science aids in the organizing of our ideas, thoughts, inquiries. There is a method to this madness called the scientific method. It involves observing, asking questions, considering routines, problem-solving, communicating and sharing decisions, exploring new things or revamping how you think about and know the natural and physical components of the world we live in.

While the importance of science in your daily lives may not always be obvious, we make countless science-based choices each day. These choices might include what to eat for breakfast, what type of gasoline to use in your automobile, or selecting the best detergent to use on your delicate textiles. Keep in mind that science is a collection of facts and figures subject to change or disapproval over time. Science has limits. It cannot provide all answers for all-natural occurrences or phenomena.

Our images of scientists and definition of learning is influenced by the common stereotype of a middle-aged white male wearing a white lab coat wearing black rounded framed eyeglasses scribbling on a chalkboard writing Einstein's equation $E=mc^2$. Doing science is not limited to the classroom or a sterile laboratory.

Doing science might involve lying down in a garden in the cool of the evening, peering into the sky counting twinkling stars and observing stars or planets wandering across the night sky. Or watching the rippling effects of throwing stones in the river or in still water forming series of concentric circles. Or maybe just sitting under the shade of bountiful fully mature fruit trees smelling their aroma and watching and naming creepy crawly things racing between bulging tree roots on the ground.

To help us understand science, it is imperative that we gain insight by starting with the first set of scientists, Adam and Eve. A scientist has been defined as a curious person who participates in thoughtful action about the world and how it behaves. Anyone can think like a scientist by asking questions, observing the world, watching and listening, and using their senses. Scientists study things and try to figure out patterns or explain how things work by repeating processes of discovery. Science in its simplest form is human efforts to understand their environment.

From this point on we shall refer to Adam and Eve as examples of our earliest scientists. Eve is the name of the first woman scientist, the wife of Adam, the mother of Cain, Abel, and Seth, and the grandmother of Enoch. Adam needed Eve to accomplish his mission in the world. Eve explored her new environment, engaging in hands-on investigations. She had to develop skills of sorting, classifying, estimating, communicating with other, even analyzing what to do next.

In Eden, God gave Adam and Eve full dominion (Genesis 1:28-30) over the entire creation. Adam and Eve were not given ownership of the world, they were given the responsibility of managing it. They were to ensure that the garden was tilled and cultivated and not abused or exploited (Genesis 2:15).

However, the time has come to rescue Eve's negative image resulting from the period when she succumbs to temptation, disobedience, and confusion. She; loses a great home and obtained a future that ended in judgment and pain. However, on the positive side, there is another side of Eve that leads to the redemption and redeemer of all humankind. Through Eve God brought human relationship, friendship, companionship, marriage into the world, and discovery through curiosity. She is the only woman recorded in scripture that had the privilege to meet and communed regularly with God in an earthly place (Genesis 3:8). While her accomplishments are not revealed in the Scriptures, we can piece together information from her environment and other things that were progressing around her.

Let's start with "In the beginning God Created.

The Bible declared that God (Jehovah Elohim) created all the materials of creations, both animate (organic substance brought to life) and inanimate (inorganic-lifeless substances) (Proverbs 26:10). Science does not know exactly where or what is the source of materials God used to create the universe. We can find in the scriptures, "That through faith we understand that the worlds were framed by the Word of God so that things which are seen were not made of things which do appear" (Hebrew 11:3). Worship points us to the purpose of creation. All things were created for God's pleasure, glory and for sincere worship. (Revelation 4:11)

First, and before any creature was, God made the universe which included the heaven and Earth out of nothing. It was necessary for God to bring materials into existence as He needed it to form things when He spoke, "Let there be." With His hands, God took one day to separate darkness and light on the earth and another day to divide the waters. Then the next day to gather the sea and cause dry land to appear. The Sun, Moon, and Stars were given rulership and purpose followed behind the creation of fish and birds. Finally, the Creator, took one more period to make large land animals and to make the man and the woman. With the satisfaction of having completed a very good work, God rested.

Everything created by God was given the power to reproduce its own kind. God created Adam and Eve in His own image and pronounced a divine blessing that they should be fruitful and multiply their own kind and fill the Earth. (Genesis 1:28). They were the source from which humankind would continue. The term "its own kind" is where groups or individuals share common traits. Everything created by God was given the power to reproduce its own kind.

The power of reproduction is not in the egg or sperm nor embryo but only in the mature parents. In the beginning, the mature parents of all living things were created with the egg, seeds, buds, and spores housed within them for future multiplication on the Earth.

Nothing could break this law of reproduction and produce any other kind naturally (Genesis 1:20-28). For example:

Breeding or a cross between a female horse, or mare, and a male donkey, or jack, will produce a mule. The horse and the donkey are different species and have differences in their number of chromosomes. A mule cannot reproduce itself. They are infertile.

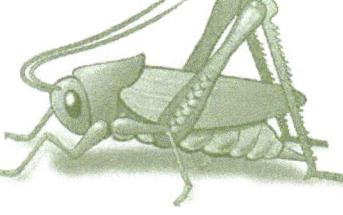

Insects are one of the largest groups of animals on Earth. There are about two million different species of insects. Each species produces its own kind. Beetles and ants do not breed naturally with each other.

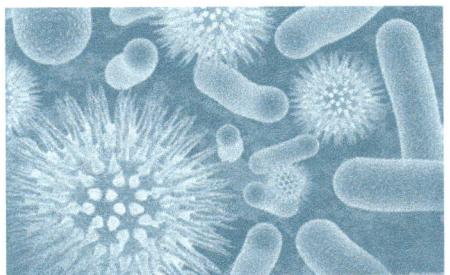

- Life multiply abundantly. Consider a tiny bacterium that can produce a population of over 280 trillion descendants in 24 hours.

- ☐ Angels living contrary to their nature and the laws of genetics established by God in the beginning.

- The outstanding characteristic about the nature of Angels is that they are not limited to our three-dimensional earthly habitats. We live in a three-spatial dimensional world with and one dimension of time. The three properties that are needed to help us find any physical location is length, width, and height. Angels are not limited to three-dimensional space because they have undefined lifespans with bodies that will not deteriorate or have bodily sickness or illnesses. Angels had the tangible spirit with bodily parts and appear as men.

- Throughout the scripture, Angels are spoken of as men. There are no female Angels on record in the Bible. The first female created in scripture was Eve (Genesis 1:27; Genesis 2:22-23). Perhaps Eve was created especially for humanity to continue in existence through the means of sexual reproduction (Genesis1:28).

- Angels as males were created as eternal beings and kept in existence without reproduction. They were created in numbers that could not be counted. They were innumerable (Hebrew 12:20). Humans were created only as a pair. Adam and Eve were commanded to reproduce and fill the Earth with their own kind. Unfortunately, Eve would have to bring forth children in pain and deep distress to fulfill this command. (Genesis 3:16)

- When humans begin to multiply on the Earth and the sons of God, fallen Angels (Revelation 12:7-10), noticed that the daughters of men were beautiful and fair to look upon. They took them as wives (Genesis 6:1-2). Angels are spiritual beings that are used as messengers of God. Jesus was the first Son of God. Jesus the Christ is the only 'begotten' son by God. No Angel could make this claim. Christ is better: "Who being the brightness of his glory and the express image of his person and upholding all things by the word of his power, when he had by Himself purged our sins, sat down on the right hand of the Majesty on high. Being made so much better than the angels as he hath by inheritance obtained a more excellent name than they" (Hebrews1:3-4).

- Righteous Angels were given the honorable positions as second sons of God. However, Christ is the second Person of the Trinity. That which is born of the 'Spirit' is a spirit (John 3:6) consequently, Adam and Eve are the third type of sons of God (Luke3:38), created lower than the Angels.

Satan's, (the adversary who was once called Lucifer in heaven) purpose was to corrupt humanity by using fallen Angels to get rid of the pure Adamite stock, which the seed of the woman Eve would bring the redeemer and the way to the redemption of sin for all (Genesis 3:15).

Hybrids in biology are the result of mixing through sexual reproduction two different species or varieties. Angels began to live contrary to their nature and mated with human women that produced children that were giants called Nephilim –giant, extraterrestrial-human hybrids (Genesis 6:4). It took supernatural elements of Satan and his fallen angels to make human offspring of such magnitude. The giants were of an abnormal size, height, extraordinarily powerful and mighty in strength (Job 16:14).

These offspring became men of honor, and authority (Genesis 6:4; Numbers 16:2). Their presence, however, increased the wickedness of the world and dissatisfied the Lord as He grieved in His heart over his creation (Genesis 6:5-7). It is recorded that some giants have six fingers on each hand and six toes on each foot. Giants have been described with having height like cedars and strength as strong oak trees (Amos 2:9-10). Hebrew spies in the land of Canaan observed the inhabitants, the sons of Anak. They were giants. In their eyes, they saw themselves like little grasshoppers among them (Numbers 13:33). The giant called King Og was thought to be 13 1/2 feet tall (Deuteronomy 3:13) and had an iron bed or coffin that was 18 ½ feet long and 8 feet wide. Goliath, the giant David the shepherd boy slew wore an armor of mail that weight 125 pounds (5000 shekels of bronze). Archeologist has often wondered if the pyramids were built by skilled Angels. Giants could now produce others of their own kind (Numbers 13:33; 2 Samuel 21:15-22). The laws of reproducing after your "own kind" was in natural operation.

Unfortunately, human fossils are quite rare and that biology and geology support the facts human remains are more capable of avoiding rapid burial in sediment and other conditions that could lead to fossilization of their remains. So, it is very rare to prove giant through fossils.

In conclusion, the giants of the Old Testament, the Nephilim, were from angelic source and were known for their mightiness which makes it is easier to accept they were the source of giant children as stated in the Bible. Modern day giants are usually awkward, uncoordinated, and endure several physical ailments, not as the described mighty men. Biologists and geneticists believe gigantism is often caused by abnormalities in chromosomes (mutated genes) or hormones. Or it can be caused by a tumor on the pituitary gland of the brain. It can cause increases in the growth of the hands, face, and feet. Also, giants became the heroes of Greek mythology.

Examining the Scripture

To help us examine the scriptures more effectively with the intent of building the character of Eve; we first need to comprehend how things are recorded in the Bible. None of the inspired authors throughout the Bible were given the complete story and outcomes of any miraculous events or prophecy. Searching the scriptures might feel like solving a 2,000-pieced jigsaw puzzle. It is best to start constructing the puzzle's border. This will give you a defined space that you will work inside as you build. Next, you can build recognized sections of the puzzle. Jigsaw puzzle pieces come in varying colors and shapes. Sometimes it is obvious which pieces will and will not fit together. As you continue to regularly work on the puzzle, you will become more familiar and recognize more quickly what will fit together.

However, the same strategies used in completing jigsaw puzzles can be applied in searching the scriptures. It is important to keep looking for the correct scripture-pieces (Psalm 119:105). You will not find all information you research on any topic or only in one specific book of the Bible. At times, you might experience some level of difficulty or frustration in interpreting what you are reading. God's word fits together and will interpret itself (Luke 24:45). The scriptures are God's word in written form for all generation to knows (2 Peter 1:20-21).

It is important that we study to show ourselves approved unto God and rightly dividing the Word of Truth. (2 Timothy 2:15). The Apostle Paul's advice to Timothy, his son in the faith, was that he should protect his spirit by avoiding vain babblings, godless discussions, and the contradictory claims of so-called "knowledge" (science) (1Timothy 6:20).

It is advisable to be patience with yourself and remember the books in the Bible are not in chronological order. The order of the books introduces you to major people, distant lands, cultures, events, and the accounts of human history. The books in the Bible are based on literature styles. The Old Testament is organized as Books of Moses (Genesis--Deuteronomy), Books of History (Joshua--2 Chronicles), Poetic/Wisdom books (Job--Song of Solomon), and Major Prophets (Isaiah—Daniel) and Minor Prophets (Hosea—Malachi). The New Testament is organized into Biographical/Gospel books (Matthew-John), Book of History (Acts), Epistles or letters (Romans-Jude) and Prophecy (Revelation).

Abracadabra: Creating Nothingness into Something

The Four Beginnings

You will find four "beginnings" starting with Genesis 1:1 to the edge of the start of Genesis 1:2. Creation was a supernatural event. It took place outside of the natural realm. These four creative acts in order are:

- Creation of Spirit beings and Angelic hosts
- Creation of the Universe
- Creation of matter
- Creation of the emergence of life

Creation of Spirit beings and Angelic hosts

All "beginnings" will lead to Adam and Eve and their impact on the future of their environment and humanity. In the creative process, science can make known objects manifestation of all things coming from the mind of God. A geological time scale is a system of the chronological dating of past events. Rocks (sedimentary, igneous, or metamorphic) formed during periods of time can serve as reference points of events during Earth's history. The large time spans of Earth's history are called eons and eras and the periods are divided into epoch and ages. Much of the permanent record source lies in the remains of fossils. Fossils are the preserved remains or traces of animals, plants, other organisms from the dateless past. The scientific study of the Earth's geological ages runs parallel with this journey back through the history of the Earth. It shows specific time period to examine ancient life climates and geography. The periods are Cenozoic (65.5 mya to the present); Mesozoic (251 to 65.5 mya); Paleozoic (542 to 251 mya); and Precambrian (4600 to 542 mya).

The world drastically changes when we enter Genesis 1:2 to Genesis 1:28. It became dark and void. This takes us to ending of the Mesozoic era with the great extinction of life on Earth and the early start of the Cenozoic era with the dinosaur (Genesis 1:25) and man as (Genesis1:26-27) co-existence (Job 40:15). Let us not go too fast. This information will be covered later in detail. Now back to the new beginnings.

The Bible declared that God (Jehovah Elohim) created all the materials of creations, both animate (organic substance brought to life) and inanimate (inorganic-lifeless substances) (Proverbs 26:10). Science does not know exactly where or what source of materials God used to create the universe. The scriptures reveal, "That through faith we understand that the worlds were framed by the Word of God so that things which are seen were not made of things which do appear" (Hebrew 11:3). Worship points us to the purpose of creation. All things were created for God's pleasure and purpose of sincere worship (Revelation 4:11).

Beginning of the Age of Angelic and Heavenly Hosts

Genesis 1:1 marks the beginning of space, time and history. But, what was happening before Genesis 1:1? What about events when there were no atoms, no time, no atmosphere, no sound, and no biological life? The Bible refers to this period as the dateless past. Before space, before time, before history, and before the material world yet good and evil existed. Let us reflect on the first "in the beginning." John states that "In the beginning was the Word, and the Word was with God, and the Word was God. He was with God in the beginning. Through Him all things were made; without Him, nothing was made that had been made. In Him was life, and that life was the light of all humankind. The light shines in the darkness, and the darkness has not overcome it." The Word refers to Christ. This is proof of His pre-existence before time (Revelation 1:8) and that He was with God. All creation came by the Son, through the Holy Spirit.

Celestial Beings - Life in the Universe

A bang is an exclamation. It is not a sound but energy that conveys the suddenness of an action or process. There was a big bang when we came to the wisdom of God pre-existence before all creation. Wisdom is needed for discernment. Discernment is defined as distinguishing someone or something with difficulty by using your sight or using your other senses. Wisdom is discerned from the Holy Spirit. The Holy Spirit gives us knowledge. Knowledge is science. God, Christ, the Holy Spirit, and Angelic hosts were all present before time at the creation of the universe. "The LORD brought me (Holy Spirit) forth as the first of his works, before his deeds of old; I was formed long ages ago, at the very beginning, when the world came to be. When there were no watery depths, I was given birth, when there were no springs overflowing with water; before the mountains were settled in place, before the hills, I was given birth, before he made the world or its fields or any of the dust of the earth" (Proverbs 8:22-26).

The word angel means messenger. Angels are also created heavenly spirit beings. The Son is the image of the invisible God, the firstborn over all creation. "For in him all things were created: things in heaven and on earth, visible and invisible, whether thrones or powers or rulers or authorities; all things have been created through him and for him. He is before all things, and in him all things hold together (Colossians 1:15-18).

Angels are glorious (Luke 9:26); immortal (Luke 20:36); powerful and mighty in the body (Isaiah 37:36). They need no rest (Revelation 4:8), can travel at inconceivable speed (Ezekiel 1:4), and they are not to be worshiped (Colossians 2:18), sing (Revelation 5:11), Holy (Matthew 25:31), ministering spirit (1 King 19:5; Psalm 104:4; Acts 12:7-11), wise (2 Samuel 14:20), subject to Christ (Nehemiah 9:6; Colossians 1:16), execute the purpose of God (Number 22:22; Psalm 103:2; Matthew 28:2), Execute the judgment of God (2 Kings 19:35 2 Samuel 24:16; Acts 12:23).

Job, the oldest book in the Bible, records the actions of Angelic beings who were present at this creative time. He received that answer from God during an interrogation. "Where were you when I laid the earth's foundation? Tell me, if you understand. Who marked off its dimensions? Surely you know! Who stretched a measuring line across it? On what were its footings set, or who laid its cornerstone—while the morning stars sang together and all the angels shouted for joy? "Who shut up the sea behind doors when it burst forth from the womb, when I made the clouds its garment and wrapped it in thick darkness when I fixed limits for it and set its doors and bars in place" (Job 38:4-10)..

What do Angels look like?

Angels are spiritual beings created by God that at times can resemble human form. They have some attributes of human such as, faces, feet, sing, eat and drink human food (Isaiah 6:1-2). Angels do not appear in the Bible as cutie cherub with wings and curly hair.

In the book of Daniel Angels are described as a man dressed in linen with a gold belt around his waist. His body was the color of Topaz and his face was like lightning. The Angels arms and legs were like burnished bronze and a vice like thunder (Daniel 10:5-6)). At the tomb of the risen Christ Angels appeared in clothing as white as snow (Matthew 28:4).

Those angels stationed near or around the throne have several pairs of wings. Their wings covered their faces to honor the holiness of God, wings over their feet while on holy ground, and wings that covered their faces because they could not look directly at God (Isaiah 6:2).

Types of Angels

There are many types of angels. It is not recorded which types were present at the creation of the universe but those that were a presence all were overjoyed at what they observed. The Angels closest to all the Holy Trinity are six-winged **Seraphim** (flaming and fiery love for God- Isaiah 6:12); many-eyed **Cherubim** (outpouring of wisdom, enlightenment, and understanding of the mysteries of God (Genesis 3:24); the **Thrones** (serve the uprightness of God's justice- Colossians 1:16). The middle hierarchy starts with **Dominions** (instruct the earthly authorities established from God- Colossians 1:16); **Powers** (fulfill the will of God- work miracle 1 Peter 3:22); **Authorities** (help people against demonic temptations- 1 Peter 3:22). And the lowest ranks are **Principalities** (have command over lower angels that direct the universe, protect lands, nations and people Colossians 1:6); **Archangels** (reveal and announce the mysteries of the faith- 1 Thessalonians 4:16); and **Angels** (are the closest to people-guide people to virtuous and holy lives, prepared to help us-1 Peter 3:22).

Six-winged **Seraphim** (flaming and fiery love for God) -Isaiah 6:12,; Isaiah 6:23; Ezekiel 1:27

Many faces-**Cherubim** (outpouring of wisdom enlightenment and understanding of the mysteries of God) -Genesis 3:24; Ezekiel 10:21; 41:18; 1 Samuel 4:4

Great flowing wheels covered with many eyes- **Thrones** (serve the uprightness of God's justice- Colossians 1:16

Dominions (instruct the earthly authorities established from God) - Colossians 1:16

Powers (fulfil the will of God and work miracles) - Ephesians 6:12; Colossians 1:6

Authorities (help people against demonic temptations) - 1 Peter 3:22)

Creation of Angelic Beings- Psalm 148:5; Job 38:7

Principalities (have command over lower angels that direct the universe, protect lands, nations, cities, towns)- Colossians 1:6

Archangels (reveal and announce the mysteries of the faith) -1 Thessalonians 4:16, Daniel 8:15-26; Jude 9

Angels- Guardians (are the closest to people- serves as guide to holy lives, prepared to help us) - Throughout the Bible from Genesis to Revelation

Grand Choir in concert in the Sky

The few names of angels mentioned in the scriptures are Gabriel (Luke 1:19-20, Luke 1:30-33), Michael (Jude 9), Lucifer (John 10:10), and Apollyon/Abaddon (Revelation 9:11). They all might have been at the celebration of the birth of the universe. "When the morning stars sang together, and all the sons of God shouted for joy" (Job 38:7). Singing express happiness and unity of emotions and admiration. They shouted for joy. It was a song of praise. Morning stars are symbolic of angels (Psalm 33:9; Jeremiah 10:12; Psalm 148:3)

Science renders us a glimpse of what they angels were shouting about as they watched the workmanship of the Holy Spirit in the creation of the universe.

"Astronomer, physicists, and asteroseisomology from all over the world have studies stars and found they can turn tiny variation in a star's light into sound. They believe that sound generated by stars are at such extreme frequencies of a trillion Hertz, six million Hertz higher than can be heard by any mammals, even bats and dolphins. Humans can hear sounds at frequencies from about 20 Hertz to 20,000 Hertz, Humans hear sounds best from 1,000Hertz to 5, 000 Hertz, where human speech is centered.

The star sound or star singing is associated with it brightness, star spin, upwelling hot gases, and descending cool gases on the surfaces creating flickers. These flickers were detected by the Kepler Space Telescope. Scientists converted the light flickering from the stars into sound. The light contained frequencies of brightness similar to sound waves but the frequencies are not audible to the human ear. Stars might be singing but since sound cannot propagate through the vacuum of space no one can hear them. www. earthsky.org

Next the Big Bang Theory!

UNQUENCHABLE ENERGY ON THE MOVE
CHAPTER 4

The universe is a huge open space. We live in the galaxy called the Milky Way. Our solar system includes our yellow Star we called the Sun, planets, and moons. The Big Bang theory suggest that the universe was created from a huge explosion billions of years ago.

Scientists think that early universe is expanding from the beginning of the explosion of the Big Bang. Some astrophysicists believe that the universe will never stop expanding while some think it will begin to shrink until it becomes a fireball again.

Beginning of Celestial Bodies-

A "bam' "conveys the abruptness of an occurrence or a sound used to imitate a hard blow. Emeril Lagasse is an American celebrity chef, author, restaurateur and television personality. During his show "Emeril Live" he would mainly wear a crisp white apron.

He taught, entertained, and engaged his live studio audience composed of ordinary people who loved to cook. They were participants as well as spectators. While he prepared his dishes, he would use his signatures catch statements, "Kick it up a notch!"; "Feel the love;" and his most popular phrase "Bam! Bam! Bam! Emeril created spice blends he called essence to reflect his personal taste. Once the ingredients were prepared, he would soon sprinkle his essence over. As he raised his arms high in the air and released the essences the audience response was electrifying excitement, overwhelming enthusiasm, applause and shouts of Bam! Bam! Bam! They wanted to see and know more. The audience shouted with great joy and proclaimed praises as an excellent chef. This also describes the reactions of the angelic hosts at the work of creation.

Cosmic Time- Big Bang or the Big Bam

Cosmology is the study of the origin, structures, and the future of the universe. On the other hand, astronomy is the study of the stars, galaxies, planets, and moons. Cosmology is theory. Astronomy is observations. The age of the universe cannot be measured directly because of astronomical distances we need to travel using the speed unit of light years. However, we use our observations of what we see repeatedly to draw more concrete conclusions and develop theories.

Scientists and astronomers from Biblical times to the present times use the mathematics, physic, technical knowledge, and their faith traditions that was practice during those times to estimate cosmic time. Cosmic time is used to describe the history and the events of the Big Bang starting with the fraction of a second of great energy release phenomena. Time then came into existence at that very moment.

The Reading the Signs in the Sky

After the birth of Jesus in Bethlehem from the east they came to Jerusalem on a quest. The three wise men refer as Magi who were Zoroastrian's priests and from the ancient Medes and Persians (the modern-day Iran) were also astronomers. They made inquiry along their route, "Where is the one who has been born king of the Jews? We saw his star when it rose and have come to worship him" (Matthew 2:1-2). The Magi were also known as star-gazers.

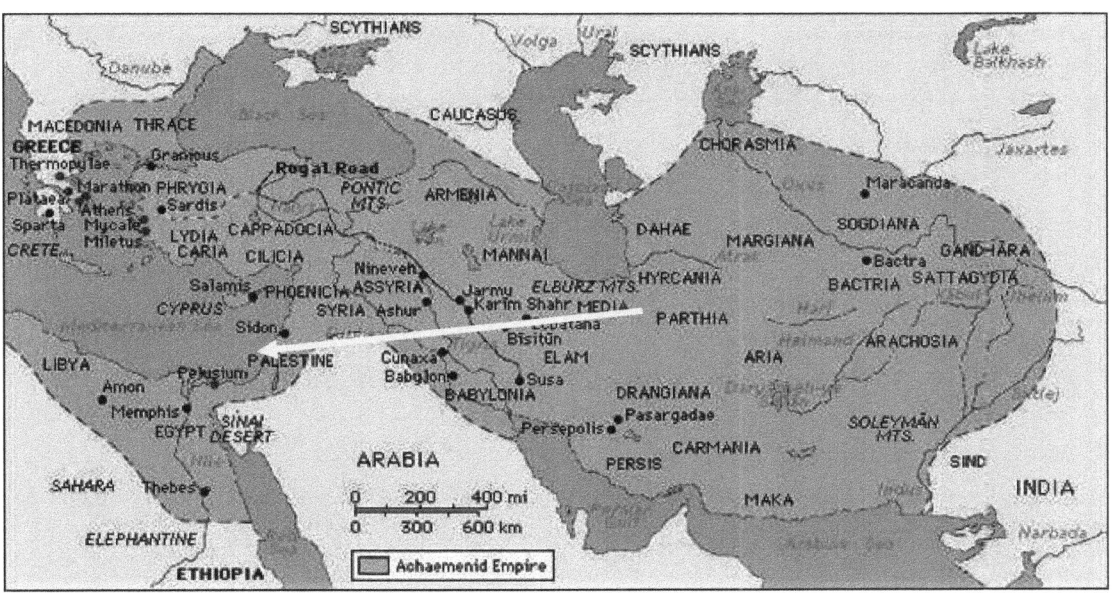

Some traditions give their names as Caspar, Melchior, and Balthasar who brought gifts of gold, frankincense, and myrrh at the birth of Jesus. They were men of great understanding. They heard of a foretold sign of a star announcing the coming king of the Jews, a Messiah, as prophesied in Hebrew writings in the Old Testament. The special star would stop when they were in King Herod's house and travel with them as they continued their journey. They studied searched, and followed the traveling star, the special celestial sign, until it stops and hovered over the place of the child's residence.

This visit is noteworthy because it marked the first time in the Bible that Jesus was recognized as a "Savior". The wise men were also called "King-seekers." These learned men would most likely share their findings along the return route to their homes. Perhaps we can assume that these early scientists, astronomers, were among the first to spread the Gospel. The Gospel being "Emmanuel" God is with us.

Another consideration is these scientists might be the first missionaries to spread the Gospel in the Eastern world. These ancient astronomers of ancient times were the first to acknowledge and worship the newborn king. The Bible states they were overjoyed (Matthew 2:7-12). Like Chef

Emeril's audience, at the birth of the universe, there was an audience of Angelic beings filled with exceeding joy over the bang in creation of the universe (Job 38:7).

Hypothetical thinking, could this extraordinary star be an Angel guide for the Magi? Stars move in orbits around the center of the galaxy. Stars are so far away from the Earth that you cannot see them move in the sky. However, they do move slowly over the sky through course of night. Stars appear to move from east to west across the night sky because the Earth is rotating so the sky is observed as rotating. Observers on Earth would see objects in the sky move counter-clockwise. A possible conclusion that can be drawn from this is the Magi were traveling from the East and saw the star in the eastern sky. As they moved west towards Jerusalem the star observably moving with them west. This would make the star moving in a clock-wise direction. Is this a case of God breaking his own natural laws by taking the star out of it natural orbit to ensure the success of the journey? Think about it!

Since ancient times, the natural laws of nature established in the beginning are still in effect. The Bible gives us the foundation for these natural laws of nature. These laws or principles were established in the beginning by God. They are binding and cannot or will not ever change. God responded to Jeremiah, "If my covenant with day and night was not in working order, if sky and Earth were not functioning the way I set them going" (Jeremiah 33:25; Psalm 104:2); "God stretches out the heaven like a canopy and spreads them out like a tent to live in" (Isaiah 40:22); "By faith we understand that the worlds were prepared by the word of God" (Hebrew 11:3). All this information or knowledge was mentioned in the Bible before the invention of high powered telescopes and satellites.

A few of the established laws of nature are:

- How thing reproduce
- How the solar system celestial objects orbit, spin, travel, and operate
- How gravity interact universally on all things
- Forms of energy do not change over time
- How the composition of form matter, elements, do not change their chemical properties
- Laws of Thermodynamics
- Essential needs of growth for all green plants
- Function of blood and breath
- Visible is the result of the invisible
- Law of biogenesis and use of stem cells

Big Bang-Age of Radiation

The universe had a beginning. Prior to the start of the universe 13.7 billion years ago, there was nothing in turns of physical matter. God is eternal and existed before time, matter, and space (Proverbs 8:22-31; Micah 5:2; Hebrew 9:14; Revelation 1:4-8). "Lord, you have been our dwelling place throughout all generations. Before the mountains were born or you brought forth the whole world, from everlasting to everlasting you are God" (Psalm 90:1-2).

The Big Bang theory states that the universe is expanding in all directions from one singular, hot, very minute, dense fire ball point in space (quantum fluctuation). A quantum is the minimum amount of any physical entity involved in an interaction of very high energy within a very small dimension of space. This superfast energy inflation is like enlargement of an atom and in seconds to the expanded size of a grapefruit.

Energy is the property that must be transferred to an object in order to perform work. There is a fixed amount of energy in the universe. Nothing can create or destroy energy. Energy can only be transformed from one form to another. Closer examination of what happens to energy released during the Big Bang cause some scientists think that stars and other elements in the universe are transforming energy while gravity continues to pull things to move away. This may be due to the force of the original Big Bang.

Imagine a rapidly expanding helium filled balloon that reaches a point that it is not able to contain the gases inside. Soon the balloon will explode. Like this balloon, the rapid expanding hot dense plasm in the universe exploded and grew and grew in a soundless explosion called the Big Bang. As the space expanded the universe cooled at rapid speeds (**inflation of the universe**) and matter formed as it interacts with gravity. The universe was now filled with space that contained electrons, photons, neutrinos. Light elements begin to form like hydrogen and helium. However, space was filled with infrared, ultraviolet rays, gamma rays, x-rays, microwaves, and other cosmic rays. There were forms of light but they are not invisible. Let us called them bands of dark light. These dark bands are located in the electromagnetic spectrum. Humans cannot see radiation or black light. However, there are animals that can detect dark light.

Humans can see reds, blues, yellows but have trouble see ultraviolet light. Some animals like dogs, cats, ferrets, bees, birds and fish can see this 'dark light' in the forms of ultraviolet radiation.

They can use the glow of ultraviolet radiation to see patterns on plants and flowers, find mates, to locate specific flowers, distinguish males from females, for finding food and finding predators. Some other animals can use infrared radiation to detect things using heat vision. Some examples of these types of heat seekers are piranha, gold fish, mosquitoes, boa constrictors and pit vipers. Butterflies are said to have the widest visual range in the spectrum of most animals.

During the Age of Radiation, it was still exceedingly too hot for light to shine. There was a period of darkness before stars and other bright objects were formed. Space was like a super-hot fog of cloud nebula. Nebula, stars birthing centers filled with gas and dust, are formed when lumps of gases began to form stars and galaxies.

Stars began to shine-Matter Dominated Era

Around one billion years ago this era involved productions of physical materials to supply the chemistry for life. These elements, carbon, hydrogen, oxygen, nitrogen, phosphorus, are needed for proteins, nucleic acids, carbohydrates and lipid. The universe space is now becoming populated with the first star formation. Stars are glowing balls of hot gases of hydrogen and helium. Galaxies are groups of billions of stars, dust and gases bound together by gravitational force. They come in different shapes. Asteroids and meteoroids are crater-covered rocks that orbit the sun. Moons are a natural satellite that orbits a planet.
Comets are dirty snowballs of ice that orbits the Sun.

Now stars began to shine. Maybe the first," let there be light!" exclamation from God occurred at the beginning of the formation of star during the Matter Dominated Era. God wanted us to have visible light. The only light frequency of the electromagnetic spectrum is visible light. The detection of light is a very powerful for observing the wonders of the universe and all creation. His desires were for the future of Adam and Eve to be able see the Stars and to read the signs of the heaven. To be able observe the wonders and glory of creation that would lead to true worship.

Visible light or white light is the part of the electromagnetic spectrum between infrared and ultraviolet. Light stimulates our sight and make things visible. Electromagnetic radiation waves are fluctuations of electric and magnetic fields which transport energy from one location to another. Light travels in a straight line through empty space. If we block the source of light from reaching our eyes, we cannot see anything. Light travels 93 million miles from the sun as a speed of 186,000 miles per second. The light we receive from the sun's surface arrives eight minutes later on earth. An important note to mention is the ultraviolet light can damage the retina of human eyes over time.

Property of Visible Light

"The lamp of the body is the eye. If therefore your eye is good, your whole body will be full of light. But if your eye is bad, your whole body will be full of darkness" Matthew 6:22-23

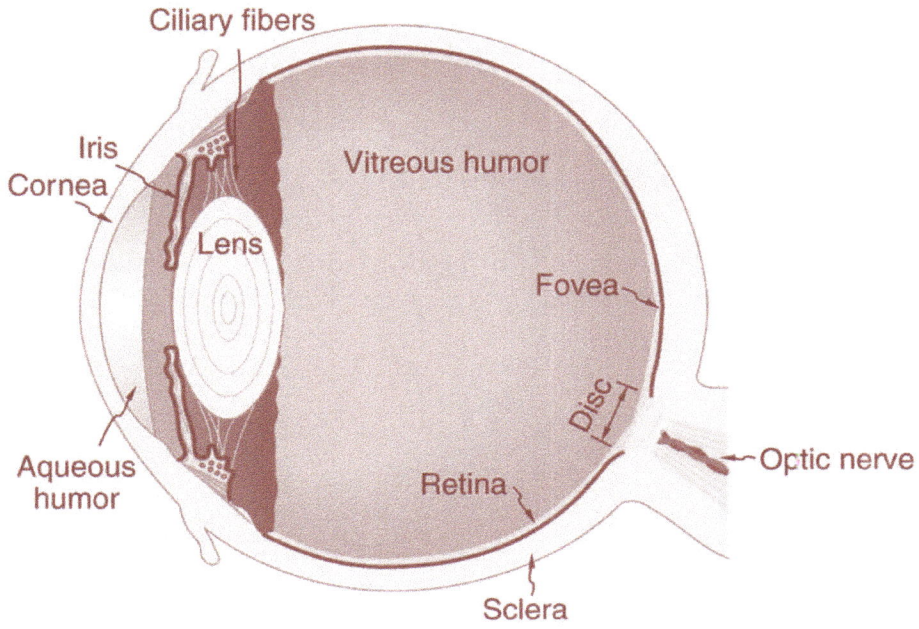

1. The sclera or white part of the eye protects the eyeball
2. The pupil, or black dot at the center of the eye, is a hole through which light can enter the eye
3. Light is focused primarily by the cornea
4. The iris of the eye functions in controlling the amount of light reaching the back of the eye by automatically adjusting the size of the pupil.
5. The eye's crystalline lens is located directly behind the pupil and further focuses light. The lens helps the eye automatically focus on near and approaching objects.
6. Light focused by the cornea and crystalline lens (and limited by the iris and pupil) then reaches the retina — the light-sensitive inner lining of the back of the eye. The retina can convert optical images into electronic signals.
7. The optic nerve then transmits these signals to the visual cortex, the part of the brain that controls our sense of sight.

Light travels in a straight line through space. Light waves can be reflected, refraction, diffracted or interfered as it enters our atmosphere.

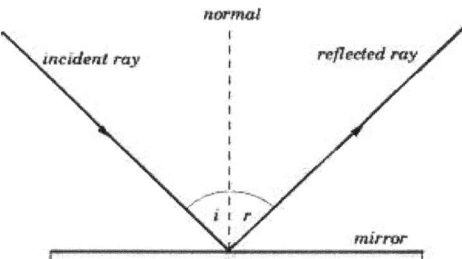

A smooth surface causes parallel light rays to be reflected in a single direction. This type of surface looks like a mirror.

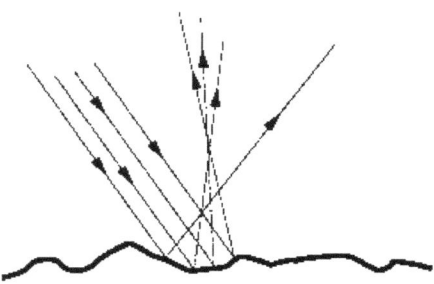

A rough surface causes the parallel light ray to be reflected in many different directions.

- Reflected - light bouncing off objects. Example is looking at yourself in a mirror

- Refraction-when light travel through different medium (liquids, gases, solids). The light's speed slows down and bend. Refraction help our eyes to see better with eyeglasses that have curve lens. The lens bends the light to focus on the retina.

- Diffracted – light spreading out in all directions. When you look between your gaps in eyelashes as you squint your eyes light will appear scatter.

- Interference – two light sources traveling together meet and one cross the other. Example is the rainbow created on a DVD or CD disc when you hold the disc up to white light.

Now that stars are in formation we see color enter the scene in the universe. White light is the mixture of different colors. We can see a rainbow of colors when white light is passed through a prism or rain drops (red, orange, yellow, green, blue, indigo, and violet). Shorter wavelength is bent more than longer wavelengths. Blue is bent more than red. Blue is always on the inside of a rainbow and red are on the outside. Colors was very important for Adam and Eve to enjoy and distinguish the fruit tree from Cedar trees, animals, birds, flowers, blue sky and white misty clouds in the Garden of Eden. Humans have high density of color sensitive cells to see vibrant colors. God knew we needed visible light before the foundation of the world was created (John 17:24).

Earth's Geological Time Scale

"In the beginning God created the heavens and the Earth" Genesis 1:1b
"The Earth is the Lord's and the fullness thereof; the world and
they that dwell therein"- Psalm 24:1

Geological time refers to physical, biological' and the environment of the Earth. Geological time scale is marked by lower rock layers called strata. This branch of geology involves the study of sedimentary and layered volcanic rocks. Geological time periods mark the origin and evolution of the Earth. The scale is divided into eons, eras, periods, epochs, and ages.

Eons	Half a billion years of more
Era	Several hundred million years
Period	One hundred million years
Epoch	Tens of millions of years
Age	Millions of years

Earth Geological Time - Origin of Earth

Geology is the study of the Earth. The Earth did not exist at the beginning of creation of the universe but was created later. Mercury, Venus, Mars, and Earth are closest to the Sun and mainly made of rocks or metals and are called the inner planet or terrestrial planets. *Terra* is derived from the Latin words for Earth so these planets composition are Earth-like. The other planets, the giant planets, are composed mainly of gases of Hydrogen, Helium, and trapped water. Extraterrestrial life is life that does not originate from Earth. It is also called space alien life. Earth is the only planet in the universe known to have "terrestrial life", life on land.

The Earth has gone through many changes and cycles which included mass extinction and Ice Ages. When the Earth began, it was hot, dry and dusty. Early planet Earth was uninhabitable due to extreme heat, collisions from other celestial bodies, radioactive elements, constant volcanic eruptions, no atmosphere, and no liquid water or water that evaporated quickly because of the heat. The surface was under continuous bombardment from meteorites, asteroids, and intense volcanism. The Earth is located within the "snow line" of the solar system. The snow line is the region close to the Sun where water is primarily in liquid or gaseous form. This location is on the outer asteroid belt between the orbit of Mars and Jupiter.

The Earth is made of four layers: liquid core (inner layer or center), mantle (the middle layer), and crust (hard outer layer-lithosphere) and the hydrosphere (is all the water on Earth including water that is trapped underground or in the atmosphere as clouds or rain).

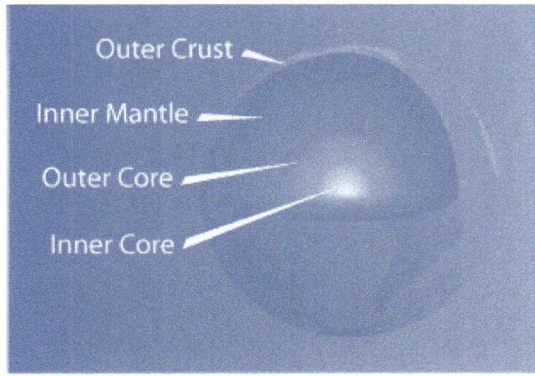

The land has many forms: mountains, hills, valleys, canyons, plateaus, plains, volcanoes, and craters. A volcano is an opening in the Earth's crust where molten rock, ashes, and gases burst forth from the mantle. Molten rock at the surface of the earth is called lava, while molten rock under the crust in the mantle is called magma. Soil is the top layer of the crust. Soil is a mixture of organic matter (decaying plants and animals) along with rock particles.

Early Atmosphere of the Earth

Meteorology is the study of the atmosphere and weather. A planet's atmosphere is the layer that surrounds that planet. An atmosphere is more likely to be retained if the gravity is high and the atmosphere is low. Without our atmosphere, there would be no life on Earth.

Earth has five layers in its atmosphere according to temperature:
- Troposphere (closest to Earth)-this is the layer weather occurs
- Stratosphere-where airplanes cruise and contain a thin layer of ozone, a protective layer shielding life on Earth from the Sun's harmful ultraviolet rays
- Mesosphere- slows down meteors that burn up before hurtling into Earth's lower atmosphere
- Thermosphere -aurora, and satellites occur in this layer
- Ionosphere- layer of electrons and ionized atoms; makes radio communications possible
- Exosphere (farthest from Earth)- begins about 400 miles above the surface of the Earth's outer space

Over very long spans of time, the heat on the new planet Earth dissipated into space, condensation and accumulation of surface water, atmosphere forming due to volcanic releasing gases.

The atmosphere is an envelope or mixture of many gases that surround the Earth. Early Earth had very little atmosphere (Hydrogen, Helium). As Earth cools a very thin atmosphere formed from gases blown out from volcanoes. The air contained hydrogen sulfide, methane, large volume of carbon dioxide, ammonia, and no free Oxygen. Scientists believed that the atmospheres of Mars and Venus are probably like the early atmosphere of Earth full of methane. When the methane gas-haze cleared, Earth's sky was blue. Oxygen was found in the compound form of water, H_2O.

Also, weather near an erupting volcano is changed. There is a lot of rain, lightning, and thunder during an eruption. This is happening because the eruption from the volcanoes released ashes and other particles, and positive and negative charged particles that attract water droplets and cause electricity to move (lightning).

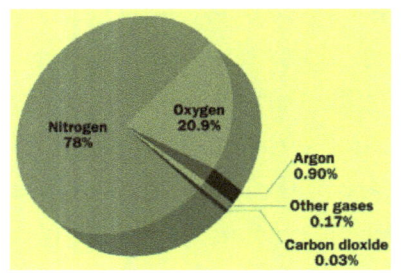

Atmospheric oxygen in the early history was the waste product of photosynthetic organisms (bacteria) and the decay of organic matter. Now conditions became ripe for the beginning of early simple life. The chemical composition of the atmosphere today is predominantly Nitrogen, Oxygen, Carbon dioxide, Argon, Neon, Helium, Methane, Krypton, Hydrogen, and water.

Age of Oxygen

Atmospheric oxygen built up in the early history of the Earth as the waste product of photosynthetic organisms (carbon dioxide + water in the presence of sunlight [radiant energy] = organic compounds [glucose] + oxygen produced by bluish-green cyanobacteria). Free oxygen in the air prepared the way for new life to emerge that used oxygen to create energy.

$$6CO_2 \text{ (Carbon dioxide)} + 6H_2O \text{ (Water)} \xrightarrow{\text{Light}} C_6H_{12}O_6 \text{ (Sugar)} + 6O_2 \text{ (Oxygen)}$$

How did Water come to Earth?

Water is essential to all life. The early atmosphere was probably mostly Carbon dioxide with little or no oxygen. There were smaller proportions of water vapor, ammonia, and methane. As the Earth cooled down, most of the water vapor condensed from ice delivered to Earth by collision of comets and asteroids formed the oceans. Earth's water increased volume due to biological processes like the water cycle (hydrological cycle). Water moves around the planet through this cycle. Evaporation from ocean and lakes, condensation forming clouds, rain refilling oceans and lakes. (Isaiah 55:9-11)

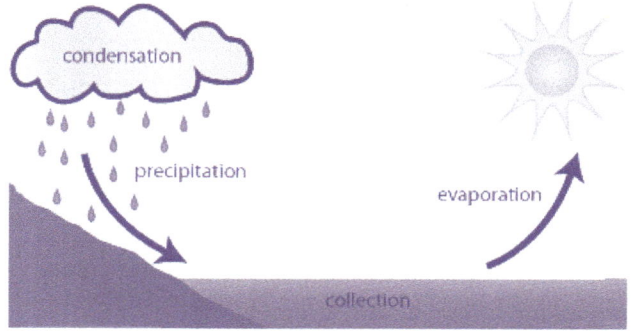

Differences in atmospheric moisture, temperatures, and pressures combined with the Earth's rotation and geographic features produce varying movements of the atmosphere across the face of the planets, and conditions we experience as weather and climate conditions in different forms of precipitation: rain, fog, snow, hail.

Our world dark with emptiness
Genesis 1:2a- Now the earth was (or became) formless and empty/ Earth was a soup of nothingness a bottomless emptiness, an inky blackness – Message Bible

Asteroids (also known as planetoids or minor planets) are believed to be left over rocks from the formation of our solar system. When an asteroid crash into Earth it is called a meteorite. They vary in size (6 feet to about 585 miles across), airless (no atmosphere), irregularly shaped (some can be spherical), pitted, cratered, rotates, revolve around the sun. Their composition consists of carbon-rich materials of rocks (containing the rare metal Iridium) and stones body.

Asteroids can be found orbiting between the planets of Mars and Jupiter. This region of orbit is called the asteroid belt. An asteroid is capable of global disaster. They can travel 150 times faster than a jet airline. If an asteroid comes too close to another celestial body (planet) it can be thrown off its natural orbit by the attraction gravitational pull. Asteroids strikes these objects can cause large amounts of dust to explode into the atmosphere resulting in the widespread loss of animal life and disrupting agriculture worldwide. Another permanent result of this disaster is the remains of huge craters. However, most asteroids are likely to burn up as they enter Earth's atmosphere.

It is believed among many geochemists and geologists that geological evidence exists that an asteroid roughly 6 miles across hit Earth about 65 million years ago, during the late Cretaceous period. It caused a high explosion (delivered an estimated energy of 420 zetta-joules, over a billion times the energy of the atomic bombings of Hiroshima and Nagasaki and left a crater of about 110 miles across off the Yucatan peninsula in southeastern Mexico. This crater is called Chicxulub. Chicxulub is the only known Earth with a remaining impact peak ring. A peak ring is a complex crater that is a type of large impact crater. It is circular depression on the surface of a planet. This depression in geology is a landform sunken or depressed below the surrounding area.

The Effects of the Impact
Kinetic energy is the energy of motion. Asteroids travel into the Earth's atmosphere at about 10-20 miles per/sec during the impact. The Law of Conservation of Energy states that energy cannot be created or destroyed but transformed into another form of energy. The kinetic energy in the speeding asteroid is transformed into explosive energy on impact. Scientists proposed that the first few hours after the asteroid influence much destruction was done to the environment of the world the possibly:
- triggered global earthquakes and volcanic eruptions

- produced dark clouds of super-heated dust, ash, and steam
- created mega tsunami causing huge vast of energy
- high volumes of carbon dioxide causing increase in the greenhouse effect
- blocked sunlight causing interruption to photosynthesis
- sulfur in the upper atmosphere causing acid rain
- alteration of the climate – maybe causing a cooling effect with block sunlight
- many plants and animals killed on the surface (large reptiles like dinosaurs died but many amphibians survived)

Scientific evidence and Meteorites impact

Fossils are the preserved remains, impressions, or traces in the Earth's crust of animals, plants, and other organisms from the geologic past. Fossils are formed in rocks and sedimentary layers (strata). Fossils found in soil layers of different ages show a record of slow, gradual changes in species, with simple organisms gradually being replaced by more complex organisms, apparently by evolutionary processes driven by natural selection or biological evolution. Natural selection is the change in heritable traits of a population overtime. This enabled organisms to better adapt to changes in their environment through transmitting the strongest genetic traits to future generations. Biological evolution is descent with modification. This involves the descent of different species from a common ancestor over many generations.

Impact discovered

In the soil layer that separates the Mesozoic Era from the Cenozoic Era, dating 65 mya, they found an excess of the element Iridium, which is common in meteorites. Meteorites are believed to be fragments of asteroids. Geochemists, believe that asteroid hit Earth at this time, and that the debris ejected from the explosion were spread in the soil layer.

Evidence for the impact events
1. The Iridium excess in the 65 mya layer has been confirmed at many points around the world
2. The same soil layer contains grains of quartz that were deformed by high shock pressures, as would occur in a giant explosion.
3. The same soil layer contains enough soot to correspond to burning down all the forests of the world. This suggests that massive fires were touched off at the time of impact
4. The same soil layer, especially around the Gulf of Mexico, contains massive deposits of tumbled boulders, as would be generated in a large tsunami, or "tidal wave." The geographic distribution of tsunami deposits suggests the impact was in the Caribbean area.
5. After a decade of searching, scientist in 1990 identified the crater associated with this material. It is no longer visible on the surface of the Earth, but is buried under sediments. It straddles the coast of Yucatan. It is revealed by mapping the strength of the gravity field over that area and by drilling. It has been dated to 65 mya.

6. Astronomers have charted numerous asteroids that have crossed Earth's orbit.

7. Craters are signs of the direct asteroid hits on Earth's surface for billions or millions of years. Because of years of erosion, it is difficult to be absolute on the sizes of the meteorites. Below in the table are ten of the earliest and largest asteroid craters on Earth.

Name	Location	Size of Diameter /Age
Vredefort Crater (world's largest & oldest known impact structure-dome)	Free State, South Africa	118 miles/ 2 billion years ago
Sudbury Basin	Ontario, Canada	81 miles / 1.8 billion years ago
Acraman Crater	South Australia	56 miles / 580 million year ago
Woodleigh Crater	Western Australia	25-75 miles / 364 million years ago
Manicouagan Crater	Quebec, Canada	62 miles / 215 million years ago
Morokweng Crater (Contained fossilized remains of the meteorite that create it)	North West, South Africa	145 million years ago
Kara Crater	Nenetsia, Russia	70.3 million years ago
Chicxulub Crater (many scientists believe that this meteorite caused or contributed to the extinction of the dinosaurs.	Yucatan Peninsula, Mexico	106- 186 miles / 65 million years ago
Popigai Crater (scientists believe carats of diamonds are in this crater- called the "impact diamonds"	Siberia, Russia	35.7 million years ago
Chesapeake Bay Crater	Virginia, United States	53 miles / 35 million years ago

What happened during the impact?

Asteroids hit Earth typically at high speeds of 10-20 miles/sec. during the impact, the kinetic energy in the asteroid (or energy of motion) is converted to explosive energy, blowing debris of dust, soil, and rocks not only into upper atmosphere, but into space, where it fell back to the top layer of the atmosphere. Much dust entered the high atmosphere that the Earth was shrouded in a dust layer that blocked sunlight for several weeks or months. This would have killed some plants, disrupting the food chain.

Other work from scientists considered for the first few hours after the impact, rocky debris would have fallen back into the high atmosphere, creating a storm of glowing fireballs in the sky. The radiant energy from these would have heated the surface to boiling temperatures for some minutes, and would have been enough to kill many animals and plants on the surface. However, in regions of heavy rainstorms or snowstorms, these organisms would have survived the first few hours. Sea creatures would have been buffered from effects in the first hours, but plankton on the surface might have died out over the weeks of darkness, decreasing the food supply for small fish, which affected the bigger fish, and so on.

These examples show how hard it is to predict the exact effects of the impact. Many species who lived on the surface (such as dinosaurs) might have been decimated in hours or weeks. Species who lived in burrows, or hibernated (like some mammals) might have survived. This may explain why mammal ruled after giant reptiles after the impact. Tiny primitive mammals may have emerged from their dens, to find that their giant reptile competition was almost gone.

EARTH'S NUCLEAR WINTER
CHAPTER 5

"Now the Earth was formless and empty, darkness was over the surface of the deep..."- (Genesis 1:2a)

"I (Jesus) saw Satan fall like lightning from heaven" (Luke 10:18)

Trouble in Heaven

The Little Big Bang

In Genesis, we do not find the details of the initial creation before Adam and Eve. However, as we search through the different books of the Bible more is revealed. The first Big Band event created four new beginning occurring between the dateless past and Genesis 1:1. These beginning were the creation of angelic beings and spiritual hosts; the beginning of the universe of energy and matter; the beginning of the physical material and inorganic world, and the beginning of organic life. It is revealed in Genesis 1:1 that God created the heavens and the Earth. There is a sudden shift in Genesis 1:2a. After the introduction of the creation of heaven and Earth a new experience of a notice a shift in that the Earth now was dark, void, and almost empty of life forms. What happened? We might consider that there was another explosion that we can call

Lucifer's Fall, Gustave Dore

the "little big bang." This event displayed opposite effects of the original Big Bang in that it was destructive power and not creative forces at work. The creative power of Genesis 1:1 brought light and life. The destructive power of 1:2a rendered darkness and death. The biblical account of this "little big bang" was caused by a cherubim angel named Lucifer and his followers.

Cherubim Angels

Cherubim are angelic beings involved in the worship and singing the praises of God. Cherubim were place at the eastern entrance to the Garden of Eden with a flaming sword flashing moving back and forth to guard the way so that Adam and Eve could not get to the tree of lie (Genesis 3:24). Lucifer was a Cherub Angel (Ezekiel 28:12-15). Perhaps Lucifer spent time with God and Christ at the creation of the universe (Job 38:7). This type of angels has been described as having four faces: that of a man, a lion, an ox, and an eagle. Each had several pairs of wings on each side. Only cherubim and seraphim are represented with wings (Ezekiel 10:5). They had straight
Feet and the soles of the feet were like the feet of calves. They sparked like the color of burnished brass of blazing fire. They had hands of a man under their wings on their four sides. Their wings were spread out upward and touching their bodies. They would move straightforward not veering off in other directions. The sound of their wings moving was like the roar of mighty rushing water. When they stood still they let down their wings (Ezekiel1:5-28).

Names of Satan

Satan, the adversary, was called Lucifer before his revolt and fall from the throne of God in heaven. He was an anointed guardian cherub that was ordained and created by God (Ezekiel 28:14). The name Lucifer comes from the Latin word *'light bearer'*, *'the shining one'* or *'son of the morning'*. The Greek meaning of this name is *'bringer of dawn for the morning star*. The Hebrew word *Satan* means the adversary, the accuser, the opponent. The Greek *satanas* transliterates Hebrew to *diabolo* which means devil. It is used as one who slanders or accuses those who trust God (Revelation 12:10).

Another name for Lucifer/Satan was the King of Tyre. Lucifer began to be proud of his own glory, perfect in beauty, and full of wisdom (Ezekiel 28:12, 17). Pride was the cause of his fall (1 Timothy 3:6). He was blameless in his ways from the day he was created until wickedness was found in him. He had everything going for him. He was in God's garden on Earth, also called the Garden of Eden. He was dressed in splendor with robe studded with jewels like ruby, topaz, emerald, beryl, onyx, and jasper, sapphire, turquoise all in setting of gold (Ezekiel 28:13-14).

Biblical Names of Satan

The Scripture describe Satan with several titles: accusers of the brethren (Revelation 12:10); serpent (Genesis 3:1); dragon (Revelation 12:9); the ruler of this world (John 12:31, 14:30); evil one (Matthew 6:13)' god of this age (2 Corinthians 4:4); Belial (2 Corinthian 6:15; roaring lion (1 Peter 5:8); liar (John 8:44); deceiver (2 Corinthians 11:3); tempter (Matthew 4:3); and the prince of the power of the air (Ephesians 2:2).

Lucifer was given dominion of the Earth (2 Corinthian 4:4; Luke 4:5-6) and he had access to heaven. He would travel from Earth to heaven on special worship celebrations. Lucifer is first mentioned in Job as Satan, as the arch enemy of God and mankind. "Now there was a day when the sons of God came to present themselves before the Lord, and Satan came also among them. Satan had conversation with God. God asked him why was he here? Satan answered the Lord, "From roaming through the Earth and going back and forth in it" (Job 1:6-9; 1 Peter 5:8).

Satan in his pride started a rebellion in heaven and was cast out (Matthew 25:14). His desires were to ascend into heaven and exalt himself above the stars of God as well as to sit upon His throne (Isaiah 14:12-14). Jesus told his disciples that he saw Satan fall like lightning from heaven (Luke10:17). We are given the warning, "Be sober, be vigilant; because your adversary the devil walks about like a roaring lion, seeking whom he may devour. But the God of all grace will perfect, establish, strengthen, and settle you" (1 Peter 5:8-10).

Science tell us that an asteroid fell onto the Earth and brought destruction. The Bible reveals Satan fell from haven to Earth and caused destruction. This is mentioned in Genesis 1:2; Jeremiah 4:23-26; and 2 Peter 3:5-6. The asteroid entered the Earth a great speed. Let us examine the speed of angels.

But first a reminder of angels' great competencies: they stand in the presence of God (Job 1:6); instruments of judgments (Revelation 7:1); bring answers to prayers (Acts 12:5-10); care for saints at time of death (Luke 16:22); gives out birth announcements of Zacharias and Mary (Luke 1:26-38); stop the shedding of innocent blood (Genesis 22:11-12); can cause earthquakes (Acts 27:23-24); and angels can be judged by God (2 Peter2:4, John 3:4, Romans 4:15; John 4:18).

Faster than a Speeding Bullet: Speed of Angels
Angels are equipped with the ability to travel with extraordinary speeds to bring us messengers of deliverance or judgement. They travel from spiritual dimension to our physical world (Judges 6:11-12; Judges 13:3-9). The speed of light in a vacuum (space) is 186,282 miles per second. As far as physicists know nothing can travel faster than light in the universe. Our Sun is 93 million away and it takes 8 minutes for the light to reach Earth after it leaves the surface of the Sun.

We draw conclusions about angel speed from the book of Daniel. "While I was speaking, and praying, and confessing my sin and the sin of my people of Israel, and presenting my supplication before the Lord my God for the holy mountain of my God. Yet while I was speaking in prayer, even the man angel, Gabriel, who I had seen in an earlier vision was caused to fly swiftly, touched me about the time of the evening oblation. And he informed me, and talked with me, and said," O Daniel, I am now come forth to give insight, skill, and understanding" (Daniel 9:20-22).

When Daniel started to pray, God instantly sent the angel Gabriel, who stands at the presence of God (Luke 1:19). The biblical hours of prayers are the third hour, the sixth hour, and the night hours of the day (9:00 AM, 12 noon, 300 PM). In the Old Testament, the hour of prayer was known as the hours of oblation or sacrifice (2 Kings 16:15; Daniel 9:21). The New Testament church went to the temple at the hours of prayer (Acts 3:1).

Light travels at incredible speeds but the Bible mentions angelic beings that travel very fast. Imagine this, the universe is 76 sextillion miles wide. This is epic and difficult to perceive. Light travel in one hour 675,000,000 miles. The evening oblation was the ninth hour. An oblation is the act of making an offering in worship or devotion. From the time that Daniel started prayer in the morning until the closing prayer in the evening was a lapse of six hours. This angel, Gabriel, traveled 675,000,000 miles time 6 hours. You do the math!

Perchance, this is how far away heaven is. Satan being one of the high-ranking angels was cast down at such great speed from heaven that he looked like lightning. Fire from the sky. Lightning is electricity. When lightning flashes, it heats gases in the air. Lightning in space do not come from clouds of water droplet. Space is a vacuum. No air. But how could lightning appear? It is produced by the clouds of other gases like sulfuric acid and cosmic dust that fill another near-by planet's atmosphere.

Storms in space are ten thousand times more powerful than ever seen on Earth as turbulence increases with friction. Under those conditions, there could have been super lightning bolts when the when the cast-out fallen angel, Satan, with his angels' streak through the space and entered the Earth atmosphere. They crashed into the surface with great speed and force. This lead to great darkness and destruction. The Bible does not indicate location on Earth where Satan fell. Imagine this scenario, the Earth shook on it axis and caused sudden violent movements of the Earth's crust leading to giant earthquakes and tremendous release of energy. Dust flew into the upper atmosphere. Black smoke and dark clouds covered the Earth. "I looked at the Earth, and it was formless and empty; and at the heavens, and their light was gone" (Jeremiah 4:23).

We might consider that Satan's rebellion happed after Earth had passed through the dinosaur age. Geologists agree something dramatic occurred between Mesozoic age; the age of Reptiles and the Age of Mammals. Something happen to change life on Earth plunged into emptiness and void. Dinosaur disappear and other smaller reptiles still exist but now mammals had the leading role.
This is the backdrop to Satan's revenge against God through tempting Adam and Eve to disobey God's instructions. They were God's new creatures that were lower than an angle but given the new stewardship over the Earth.

Now for the renewal work to begin (Genesis 1:2b). "When you send your Spirit…and You renewed the face of the Earth" (Psalm 104:30).

CHAPTER 6
RENEW, RESTORE, REPLENISH

The Holy Spirit is a mighty force that emanates from God and his Son, Jesus. The Holy Spirit acts as the workman that executes and accomplishes the plan or will of Elohim, the creator of all, and His Son, Jesus the Christ. God sent his Spirit purposefully (Psalm 33:6-9). The Spirit of God is everywhere (Psalm 139: 7-10). If God did not send forth His Spirit, there would have been neither a creation nor a renewing of the Earth. The Earth would have remained in a state of judgement and devastation (Psalm 104:30). In a scientific way the Holy Spirit is powerful source of energy that keeps a system working. We cannot see this energy but we will have the evidence of its operation.

Day One-Setting Off Spiritual Dynamite

"Earth was a soup of nothingness, a bottomless emptiness. God's Spirit brooded like a bird above the watery abyss"- Genesis 1:2 Message Bible

Genesis 1:2- Nuclear Winter

Now the earth was formless and empty, darkness was over the surface of the deep, and the Spirit of God was hovering over the waters (Genesis 1:2)

God's judgment on the Earth involved a devasting global flood followed by an Ice Age. All life on planet Earth was mostly extinguished. The age of the Earth and the extensive fossils showing development over extended periods of time relate to this first Creation. The sea was close to freezing into a permanent solid mass if the Spirit of God had not intervened and hovered over the waters.

This condition is called a nuclear winter or atomic winter resulting from hundreds of nuclear bombs released on Earth. Nuclear winter is the severe global climatic cooling effect that occurs after several firestorms. A feature of these storms is a fire with its own storm-force winds. This force is like the atomic bombing of Hiroshima and Nagasaki, Japan. The firestorms are combined with high doses of radiation fallout that will interfere with green plant photosynthetic process, destroy portions of the ozone layer. Ultraviolet rays would kill marine life and blind animals on land.

The conditions described in Genesis1:2 resembles the same conditions of a nuclear winter in which layers of dust and smoke blocking the Sun's rays. The term "nuclear winter "was coined to describe the effects nuclear wars would have on Earth's atmosphere if Hydrogen bombs had exploded all over the Earth. The Earth would be completely cut off from the Sun's warming. Next, a worldwide darken of the atmosphere. The result would be a terrible, planet- wide winter. The Earth would be so cold and dark that all life would cease to exist.

Nuclear winter might explain why the wooly mammoths were frozen so quickly that many had food still in their mouths. That has always been a puzzle as to how or why they became frozen so quickly and suddenly. Research indicates many species disappeared over night, geologically speaking. Somewhere between 10,000 and 8,000 years ago we lost mammoths, saber-toothed tigers, giant armadillos, and other animals. The best current scientific theory is violent climate changes.

Energy is the ability to do work. Energy exerts a force on an object. You cannot see energy, but you can see the effects it produces. Energy can be classified as two types: either potential or kinetic energy. The root of energy is *energia*. Energia is the manifestation of energy being transferred from one physical system to another. It is expressed as the product of a force and the distance it moves a body in the direction of that force. This is a thermodynamic definition of work.

Kinetic energy is moving energy. Potential energy *(potenziale - chemical energy by position)* is energy at rest or stored for later use. Potential has the capacity to do something. It is energy waiting to be used. Mechanical energy is equal to the sum of potential energy and kinetic energy.

What first comes to mind when you hear on the news that an office building is going to be demolished. The words excavation, explosion, TNT, or dynamite will most likely enter your thoughts. We sometimes call a person that has a lively personality a "dynamite person".

An explosion consists of a release of potential energy in a chemical compound transformed into kinetic energy. A common source of explosive materials are dynamite sticks. Dynamite is a very explosive compound made of nitroglycerine in a tube. The tube needs a blasting cap to detonate a small explosion inside the tube that triggers the final, larger explosion. Once ignited, the reaction will proceed extremely rapidly.

Brooding and Hovering over the Deep

In the Greek language, *dunamis* meant the ability to achieve in physical, military, or political power. The Hebrew for *dunamis* signifies power or a great force. In the Gospel (Matthew, Mark, Luke, John) and Acts *dunamis* signifies the power of God. Dunamis can also refer to inherent power, power residing in a thing by its nature or which a person or thing exerts and put forth (Matthew 22:29; Matthew 24:30).

The Spirit of the Lord was the workman in creation (Proverbs 8:22). By His Spirit, the heaven (universe) was adorned (Job 26:13a). The Spirit of the Lord, also known as Holy Spirit or Holy Ghost, is a source or an input of divine energy. For all systems to work there must be an input of energy. And the Spirit of God moved upon the face of the waters" (Genesis 1:2b) and great changes took place.

The Hebrew *rachaph* means to brood, relax, to flutter, to shake. The Hebrew writing that indicated movement was synonymous to brooding or hovering, as when a mother bird broods (warms, protects, or covers) over her eggs to bring forth new life. There was a situation in early Earth that was lifeless, waste, and void all over the surface. There was darkness upon the depth of the water. Then the Spirit of God came to brood, to hover, to shake things up so that this situation became less hostile and more acceptable to produce life. The Holy Spirit moved with a force that blasted out anything, not in the plan of restoration. The Spirit was breaking

up the products of judgement into transformation of a new Earth. God brings life into the world through His Spirit of renewal and creation. Very much like lightning striking an object electrifying and transforming its nature.

A glimpse of omnipotence of the Holy Spirit

- Like **Fire**: consuming fire (Hebrew 12:29); burning bush (Exodus 3:2); Shekinah glory (Exodus 14:19)
- Like the **Wind/Breath of God**: (Gk. *Pneuma*- a current of air or breeze = a Spirit; Heb. *ruach* – breathe, air in motion= breath= life= Spirit) The divine energy (Psalm 33:6-7; John 20:21-22; Psalm 150: 6, Job 33:4)
- Like **Water**: cleansing – (Matthew 3:11; John 3:5)
- Like a **Dove:** peaceful and pure- Luke 3:22; Mark 1:10; Matthew 3:16
- Like **Oil**: uniting us with Christ- Acts 10:38; 1 John 2:20-27
- Like a **Cloud**: leading the way and protection- Exodus 16:10
- Giving **Authority** (Gk. *exousia*) authorization of an officer or a messenger to carry out specific task. God has passed on his authority to us through Jesus who sent the Holy spirit to continue his ministry through us. (Mark 1:21-28; Acts 1:8; Luke 10:19)
- **Maintenance of creation**: (Psalm 104:29-30)
- Like **moving Energy**: sound like thunderous clapping noise, wind, fire (Act 2; 1 Corinthian 2:4)
- **Life giving**: miracle of the Spirit hovering over virgin Mary and the miraculous conception of Jesus- (Luke 1:35); Man was formed out of the dust and became animated dust after the breath of God entered him (Genesis 2:7)
- **God's invisible qualities** – His eternal power and dive nature (Romans 1:20)
- **All surpassing power from God** – 2 Corinthian 4:7
- **His (God) power is at work within us**- that can do immeasurably more than we ask (Ephesians 3;20-21)

Restoration and Renewal of the Earth

The Earth had experienced drastic climate changes after the rebellion and fall of Satan. Satan and his angels' rebellion may have occurred after the Earth had passed through the dinosaur age. Geologists agree that something dramatic occurred between the Ages of Reptiles and the Age of Mammals. This is one of the most puzzling events in the history of life on Earth and an untested hypothesis to what caused the changes from the Mesozoic Age.

Planet Earth was cold and dark. The Sun could not penetrate the darkness in the atmosphere. All radiant energy was blocked out by dark clouds. Then an Ice Age began. The *dunamis*, power of the Holy Spirit hovered and began to warm and renew the Earth. The brooding of the Holy Spirit melted the ice and created massive flooding. he waters settled in the low areas revealing the land. The *dunamis* property of the Holy Spirit started a stirring or mixing to create a solution of elements into nutrients in the water needed to form simple components for life. Agitation of the water was made by the Spirit like an eagle stirring up its nest (Deuteronomy 32:11, Isaiah 45:18).

The Oceans and Mixing the Primordial Soup

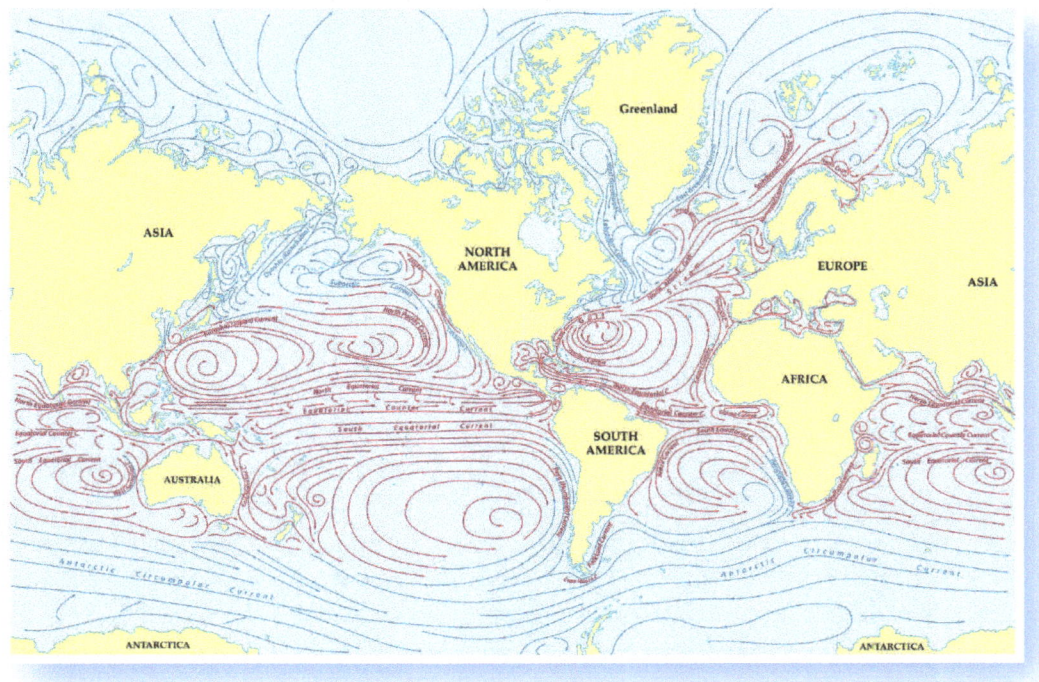

Perhaps this is the origin of the scientific explanation or theory of the origin of life, a primordial soup. The theory was generated separately in the 1920s by the Russian biologist Alexander Oparin and the English geneticist John Haldane. Basically, the theory states that when energy, in the form of lightning, heat, or ultraviolet radiation, was added to Earth's early atmosphere and gases in the ocean, the basic building blocks of life were created.

The primitive oceans of the Earth became a homogenous solution, rich in organic compounds. Simple building unit were formed. The Holy Spirit hovering over the water releasing energy (maybe some lightning) causing wind to blow. These created waves of turbulence provided and more opportunity for the water to circulate and absorb gases.

As the planet Earth warms the ocean, as compared to the land, it holds most of the extra energy it receives. Thermal (heat) energy conducts the transfer of heat by mean of molecular excitation. The heat transfer changes the internal energy of both the atmosphere and the ocean. Geologists and Astronomers proclaims that meteorites that bombarded the Earth's surface might have contained atoms of Phosphorus, Nickel, and Iron along with gases from the atmosphere Methane, Helium, Hydrogen, Oxygen, Nitrogen, and Carbon.

Formation of Organic Molecules

Organic Elements of Life

Two or more atoms of the same elements (C, H, O, P, N) chemically join or bond together and begin to form molecules. Molecules of different elements chemically join or bond together to form compounds. Scientists support the idea that molecules began to rearrange to produce the first organic compounds amino acids. Amino acids are the building blocks of proteins that later produced enzymes, and hormones, and the bridge to nucleotides the building blocks of nucleic acids (DNA, RNA, ATP), the genetic material of life and the energy bonds for living things.

Later, we get bonding of other carbon compounds that supported the formation of glucose, the six-ringed carbon compound that build into carbohydrates, the primary energy source. Lipids the building blocks of fats, cell membrane, and cell parts bonded. These building blocks (monomers) bond to from large molecules (polymers) that gave rise to life and organisms. The organization of life is atoms into molecules; then cells into tissue into organ into organ system into organism.

Stirring the Soup

The ocean operates on a system like a conveyor belt, moving things around. The wind driven over the surface of the ocean created currents that caused circulation of warm water towards the poles and colder water toward the equator. In fact, the Great Ocean Conveyor belts of the Atlantic Ocean move warm (or heated water from the Sun) north towards the poles. Up north the heavier cold water near the poles sinks very deep and spreads out all around the world. The sinking water is replaced by warm water near the surface. This moves all the enriched elements around the globe.

The brooding of the divine energy source, the Holy spirit, brought forth Earth to produce life.
Now Earth needed light and air to substance new life.

God Speaks! It happens!

The Hebrew term for create is *bara* which means to bring into being. The universe is brought into existence in (Genesis 1:1; Job 38: 4-7). Great sea creatures and winged birds were created as stated in Genesis 1:21). Next, Man is created out of the dust found in Genesis 1:27. All other references are God made (Hebrew *asah*- to produce out of already existing material), ***saw, divided, and called***. This gives credibility to the work of the six days as mainly reconstructive and renewal.

The Sun, Moon, Stars, Earth and other planets, waters, darkness, and light have already been created before day one. Now God chose to restore Earth because the heavens were commanded to withhold light (Jeremiah 4:23-26).

The 21st century opened with a culture that is inundated with words. Words are units of language

They serve as a principal carrier of meaning, consisting of one or more spoken sounds or combination of sounds, or appearing in their written format.

Words, words, and more words. We text, we tweet, send emails, Facebook, and some of us still write letters. Words have power and authority. Words can heal, hurt, humor, or even destroy. God spoke the world into existence with just a few utterances. "By faith, we understand that the universe was formed by God's command so that what is seen was not made from what was visible" (Hebrews 11:3). Speaking creates intimate relationships with the listener.

God's Word is authoritative and powerful.

God:
- **Said** – name or mention before, utterance to convey information or intention
- **Saw**- to perceive, understand, to see
- **Divided** – separate into parts
- **Called**- cry out, cry out to someone, holler, shout, call
- **Made**- formed in a place to bring into existence by shaping or changing material, to cause to happen
- **Set**- put or bring into a specified state, or position
- **Blessed** – made holy, consecrated to protect, give a benediction
- **Create**-bring something into existence, originate, bring about, generate
- **Ended**-to bring to an ultimate point, finish, perform a final act
- **Rested**- cease work or movement to relax, refresh, recover strength
- **Sanctified**- declare holy, purify, hollow, blessed

Speak a Word

When God created the first human beings, Adam and Eve, they were fully formed and functional

adults. They were capable of thinking, interacting, reproducing, and speaking. He created them in His own image, *Imago Dei* (Genesis 1:26-27). God spoke to this couple from the very beginning of their existence (Genesis 1:28-30). Adam and Eve had the ability to speak and make decision on the very day that they were brought into existence. We need our voices every day to enable us to interact in our community. We mainly speak without even thinking about it.

It takes the first ten years of a child's life to develop speech patterns and voice control like that of an adult. Speaking is mainly accomplished through the respiratory system. This involves muscular actions and a series of cavities or chambers: nasal cavity, sinus cavity, mouth cavity, and the chest cavity.

Conversation with Talking Animals

Adam was given the gift to communicate with others through speech. Other creatures in the animal kingdom are not anatomically or physiologically designed to speak but do make sounds. Only two animals were granted for a brief period the gift to communicate with humans through speech.

A snake (serpent) who was deceitful and a donkey, who was attempting to protect it, owner. The first incident of an animal taking was in the garden of Eden. It involved a snake (serpent) talking to Eve. He lied and tempted Eve that she could eat that which was forbidden with no consequences.

He tempted her with a sly insinuation that she could be like a god, knowing good and evil (Genesis 3:1-5; 2 Corinthians 11:3).

The second incident was when the Prophet Balaam was the son of Beor, a king of Edom (Genesis 36:31-32). The prophet had the reputation of being able to pronounce a curse or blessing upon people. He was called by Balak, king of Moab, to curse Israel and was offered a reward (Numbers 22:5-6).

God told him to bless and not curse Israel. But, he failed to replay this new message that God told him he could not curse but must bless Israel.

Balaam sought to persuade God to cooperate with him, through repeated sacrifices, so he could get the reward (Number 22:19). On the road or path, he traveled, "The angel of the LORD stood in a narrow place where there was no way to turn to the right hand or the left. When the donkey saw the angel of the LORD, she lay down under Balaam; so Balaam was angry and struck the donkey with his stick. First, the angel is seen only by the donkey Balaam is riding. The prophet was rebuked by this donkey for his sin and transgression and gave him a startling warning of pending life and death. And the LORD opened the mouth of the donkey, and she said to Balaam, "What have I done to you, that you have struck me these three times? Am I not your donkey upon which you have ridden many times? Why do you keep beating me?" (Numbers 22:22-33;2 Peter 2:16)

The shape of the mouth cavity, formation of the tongue, irregular arrangement of the teeth, the jaw bones of the donkey were not designed for speech. It was the wonder of God that she spoke. "For with God, nothing shall be impossible." (Luke 1:37).

God Puffs Life into Adam

"Who has made man's mouth?" (Exodus 4:11a)

Adam and Eve needed the breath of God to speak and communicate with Him and each other. To make sounds and to speak we need a power source, a vibrator, and a resonator. The body parts and spaces that work together to produce sounds we make when we speak and sing are our lungs, larynx, and our throat, nose, mouth, and sinuses.

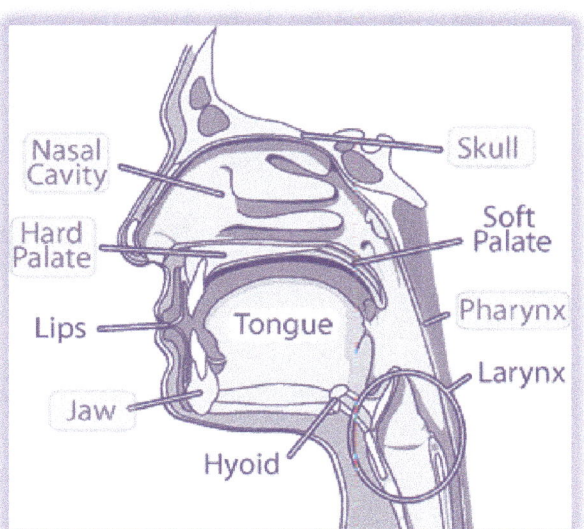

To ensure clear sounds are being made, you need a power source for your voice. This source of power is the air you exhale and inhale from your lungs.

Airstreams or controlled puffs of air from our lungs are released and blown through our larynx (voice box). The larynx sits on top of the windpipe. The diaphragm expanding and abdominal muscles help to push the air out the lungs. Your breath supports your sound.

Stretched across the top of the windpipe are the vocal chords, which consists of two folds. When we expel air from the lungs and push it through the larynx, the vocal chords vibrate from the flow of the airstream. This makes sounds. The frequency of these vibrations determines pitch.
Pitch is the degree of highness or lowness of a tone produced by the rate of vibrations on the cords. Pitch is determined by the length and tension of the vocal folds. Smooth vibrations help you to make pleasant or soft sounds.

The throat, nose, and mouth, tongue and teeth make up chambers that serve as a resonator system. The resonator adds richness and tone to your voice that give you your voice distinct character.
Anything that affects your breath will affect your sound making. For example:

- Breathing in smoke from fireplace, cigarettes, pipes, and illegal drugs can dry out the throat
- Hydration keeps your voice from tiring quickly
- Drinking alcohol, caffeine, and even artificial sweeteners can cause vocal problem, especially for singers.
- Sleep deprivation
- Air conditioning, fans, and heating sources
- Colds, flus,
- Allergies
- Some dairy products can cause phlegm and interfere with speaking or singing

And God Said.

"For the word of the LORD is right, and all his works are done in truth. He loves righteousness and judgement: The Earth is full of the goodness of the LORD. By the word of the LORD were the heavens made, and all the starry host by the breath of His mouth" (Psalm 33:4-6).

The first voice we hear in the Bible is God saying (He spoke), "Let there be light!" (and it happened). Each act of creation and restoration began with a word from God. God's word has the power to create, redesign, rearrange, or change matter both chemically and physically. Energy input is needed initiate all systems to start. God's word is potent and transforming.

Let there be:

1. And God said, "Let there be light" (Genesis 1:3)
2. And God said, "Let there be a firmament in the midst of the waters and let it divide the waters from the waters" (Genesis 1:6)
3. And God said, "Let the waters under the heavens be gathered together unto one place, and let the dry land appear." (Genesis 1:9)
4. And God said, "Let the Earth bring forth grass, the herb yielding seed, and the fruit tree yielding fruit after his kind, whose seed is upon the Earth." (Genesis 1:11)
5. And God said, "Let there be lights in the firmament of the heaven to divide the day from the night; and let them be for signs, and for seasons and for days, and years" (Genesis 1:14)
6. And God said, "Let the waters bring forth abundantly the moving creatures that have life and fowl that may fly above the Earth in the open firmament of heaven" (Genesis 1:20)
7. And God said, "Let the Earth bring forth the living creature after his kind cattle, and creeping thing, and beast of the Earth after his kind" (Genesis 1:25)
8. And God said, "Let us make man in our image, after our likeness; and let them have dominion over the fish of the sea, and over the fowl of the air, and over the cattle and over all the Earth and over every creeping thing that creeps upon the Earth" (Geneis1:26).

When God speaks His word and desires will be accomplished and achieved the purpose for which they were sent. "You will go out in joy and be led forth in peace, the mountains and hills will burst into song before you, and all the trees will clap their hands. Instead, the thorn bush will grow the juniper and instead of briers the myrtle will grow. This will be for the Lord's renown for an everlasting sign, that will endure forever" (Isaiah 55:10-12). God said to Jeremiah the prophet about the judgment on the false prophets and their sins, "Is my word like as a fire (a great purifier that remove the impurities from metals and leaves only the pure form of the metal) and like a hammer that breaks a rock in pieces (crushing evil and results in strengthen the heart)" (Jeremiah 23:28-29).

Seven facts about the Word of God are, "For the word of God is (living and active) quick (Greek *zao*- full of vigor, rapid response), and powerful (Greek *energes*- effectual), and sharper (Greek *tomoteros*) than any two-edged sword (Greek *machaira*), piercing (to penetrate) even to the dividing asunder of soul and spirit and of the joints and marrow, and is a discerner (to recognize, made clear) of the thought and intents of the heart (Hebrews 4:1).

Symbols of the Word of God

1.	A hammer to convict -Jeremiah 23:29
2.	A Fire to refine -Jeremiah 23:29
3.	A mirror to reflect James 1:23
4.	A seed to multiply - 1 Peter 1:23
5.	A laver to cleanse - Ephesian 5:26
6.	A lamp to guide - Psalm 119:105
7.	Rain and snow to refresh – Isaiah 55:10
8.	A sword to cut – Hebrew 4:12, Ephesian 6:17
9.	A bow for revenge Habakkuk 3:9
10.	Gold to enrich Psalm 9:7-10
11.	Power to create faith Romans 10:17
12.	Give eternal life – 1 Peter 1:23
13.	Food to nourish: milk for babes -1 Peter 2:2; Bread for the hungry-Matthew 4:4; Meat for men -Hebrew 5:11-14; Honey for dessert – Psalm 19:10
14.	Trumpet – symbol of God's voice – Psalm 29:3, Psalm 68:33
15.	Thunder – symbol of God speaking – Exodus 19:19, Revelation 8:6

Modified source: Dakes Reference Bible, page 433

Brain connection to Speech

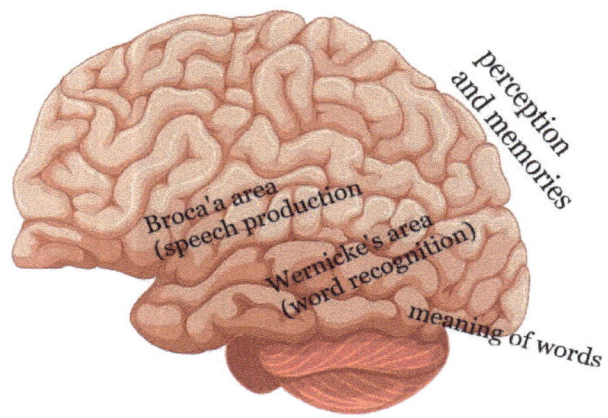

The size of the human brain and the nerve impulse or neuron connections that enable humans to speak. To speak a word that has been read, information is obtained from the eyes and travels to the visual cortex of the brain.

From the visual cortex, information is transmitted to the posterior speech area called the Wernicke's area. From there information travels to Broca's area and then to the motor cortex to provide the necessary muscle contraction to produce the sound. To speak a word that had been heard, we must invoke the primary auditory cortex, not the visual cortex.

The Apostle Paul warns us not to use unwholesome words out of our mouth (Ephesians 4:29). Cancel words of vulgarity, dirty jokes, foul language. Use words that will benefit those who listen. We open our mouths to praise and glorify God (Romans 10:9-10).

When Jesus spoke, things also happened !

The Faith of the Centurion

"When Jesus had entered Capernaum, a centurion came to him, asking for help. "Lord," he said, "my servant lies at home paralyzed, suffering terribly." Jesus said to him, "Shall I come and heal him?" The centurion replied, "Lord, I do not deserve to have you come under my roof. ***But just say the word,*** and my servant will be healed. For I am a man under authority, with soldiers under me. I tell this one, 'Go,' and he goes; and that one, 'Come,' and he comes. I say to my servant, 'Do this,' and he does it. When Jesus heard this, he was amazed and said to those following him, Truly I tell you, I have not found anyone in Israel with such great faith" (Matthew 8:5-10).

Jesus Speaking to the Wind

"As they sailed, He fell asleep, and a squall came down on the lake so that the boat was being swamped, and they were in great danger. The disciples went and woke up Jesus saying, "Master, Master, we are perishing!" Then Jesus got up and rebuked the wind and the raging waters, and they subsided, and all was calm. "Where is your faith?" He asked. Frightened and amazed, they asked one another, "Who is this? He commands even the winds and the water, and they obey Him!" (Luke 8:23-25)

The Power of Speech
The First and Last recorded spoken statements of God, Adam, Eve, Serpent, and Jesus

1. First recorded words of God (Elohim) was "Let there be light" (Genesis 1: 3).

2. The first recorded words of Adam were about the new creation, the woman. And Adam said, "This is now bone of my bones, and flesh of my flesh: she shall be called Woman because she was taken out of Man" (Genesis 2:23).

3. First recorded words of the serpent. Now the serpent was subtler than any beast of the field which the LORD God had made. And he said unto the woman, ", Did God said, you shall not eat of every tree of the garden?" (Genesis 3:1)

4. Eve's first recorded words placed her in a conversation with the serpent about God's commandment against eating the forbidden fruit. And the woman said unto the serpent, "We may eat of the fruit of the trees of the garden "But of the fruit of the tree which is in the midst of the garden, God said, we shall not eat of it, neither shall we touch it (forbidden), lest we die" (Genesis 3:2-3).

5. Last recorder words of the serpent. And the serpent said unto the woman, "You shall not surely die: For God does know that in the day that you eat thereof, then your eyes shall be opened, and you shall be as gods, knowing good and evil" (Genesis 3:4-5).

6. Last words of Adam were that of blame and confession. And the man said, "The woman whom you gave to be with me, she gave me of the tree, and I did eat." (Genesis 3:12)

7. Last recorded words of Eve were one of Praise to God. "And Adam knew his wife again; and she bare a son, and called his name Seth: For God has appointed me another seed instead of Abel, whom Cain kill" (Genesis 4:25).

8. The first recorded words of Jesus in the Gospel found him as a boy, 12 years old, in the temple teaching. "Why were you searching for me?" he asked. And He said to them, "Why did you seek me? Did you not know that I must be about My Father's business? But they did not understand the statement which He spoke to them" (Luke 2:49-50).

9. The last recorded words of Jesus from the cross. And when Jesus had cried with a loud voice, he said, 'Father, into thy hands I commend my spirit': and having said thus, he gave up the ghost" (Luke 23:46).

Time Began- Let there be Light

The Sun, Moon, Stars, Earth and other planets, waters, darkness, and light have already been created before day one. Now God chose to restore Earth because the heavens were commanded to withhold light,

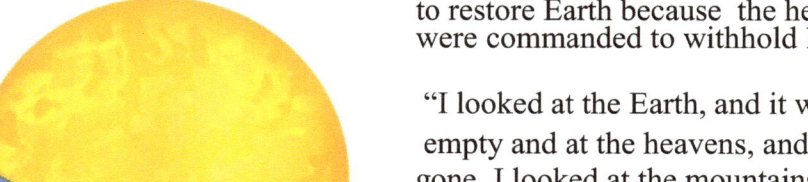

"I looked at the Earth, and it was formless and empty and at the heavens, and their light was gone. I looked at the mountains, and they were quaking, all the hills were swaying "(Jeremiah 4:23-26). The renewing of the Earth was necessary because of the terrible cataclysm that had wiped all life was responsible for plunging he planet into frozen darkness like a star (meteorite) falling from the sky.

Genesis one verse three opens with God making a divine imperative statement, "Let there be Light!". God inspected the light and was satisfied for it was good. Then He divided the light and darkness distinct from each other in all parts of the Earth. God called the light Day and the darkness he called Night. And the evening and the morning were the first day. This was the reappearance of light from the Sun on the Earth since the judgement of Lucifer and his fall from heaven.

The study of the behavior and interaction of light with other matter is known as optics. Optics usually describes the behavior of visible, ultraviolet, and infrared light. In physical terms, 'light' is applied to all the electromagnetic spectrum groups of wavelengths. Radio waves, microwaves, infrared, white light, x-rays, gamma rays are the wavelengths that make up the spectrum.
Regardless if the wavelengths are visible or not to human eyes all wavelengths are called light. Let us loosely refer to all the light frequencies as dark light except white light waves that is also called visible light. White light is a very small portion of the spectrum. It is the only portion of the spectrum that the human eyes can detect.

During the time of Adam and Eve and the biblical world, visible light was the only known part of the spectrum because everyone could see the sunlight or sunrays. Light is essential to Earth. It makes God's creative works visible and life possible. It provides heat and energy for plants, animals, and humans. Without the light from the Sun green plants and some bacteria would not be able to enter photosynthesis and produce oxygen and glucose that animals and humans need to live.

Light has a dual personality. It acts as a wave and like a particle. Light travels in a straight line and can be reflected, refracted, and absorbed. White light can be separated into colors. The Sun and other Stars are our sources of white light. The speed of light is 186,000 miles per second in a vacuum (space). The letter 'c' is used to denote light. 'C' origin is Latin from the word *celeritas* meaning swiftness, constant, or speed. Light is the fastest moving energy we know of in the physical world.

Another form of light is living light called bioluminescence. It is a biochemical reaction in which animals in their cells can creates light without heat. Animals deep in the dark oceans and on Earth used this light to communicate or attract a mate.

Times Flies

God commanded the Sun, Moon, and Stars to divide day and night instituting forever natural laws that will never change. The day and night established reoccurring periods of certain amounts of lightness and darkness. The separation of light and darkness gave way to position or location, usage, distance, and space of celestial bodies interactions with Earth. This was the beginning of periods of time.

One hemisphere of the Earth would be light while the other hemisphere is dark. All of this happen by motion. This motion is referred to as rotation. Rotation is Earth making a complete spin on its axis, an imaginary center spindle running through the North and South Poles. This rotation is completed every twenty-four hours. The Earth is spinning on it axis during this period of motion bringing about day and night. One Earth day is 24 hours.

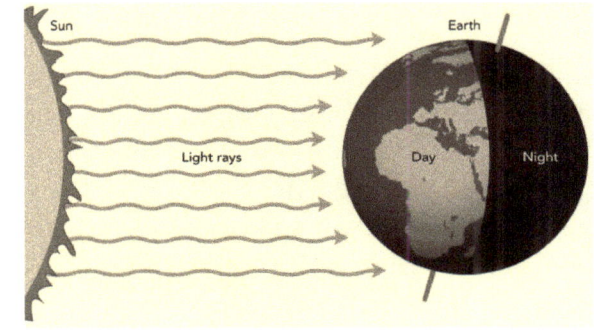

When and why there is Night/Evening?

Night starts when the sun disappears below the horizon. The horizon is the line that separates the land from the sky. Some light stays in the sky for a while, this time is called dusk. Dusk is the time after the sun goes below the horizon when there is still sunlight in the sky (Numbers 9:3; 2 Kings 7:5). Night ends when the Sun peeks above the horizon. There may already be some light in the sky even before the sun moves above the horizon. This time is called dawn. Dawn is the time before the sun rises above the horizon, when there is sunlight in the sky (Matthew 28:1; 2 Peter 1:19). The light you see at dusk and dawn is called twilight. Twilight is the light that is visible in the sky at dawn and dusk, when the sun is below the horizon (Job 3:9; Job 24:15; 1 Samuel 30:7; 2 Kings 7:5-6). Noon is when the Sun is in the exact center of the sky. Also called "high noon" because the Sun is at its highest point in the sky (Genesis 43:16; Deuteronomy 28:29).

The length of night depends on where you are located on the Earth. Nights can be long or short or equal to day hours. The Earth orbits or revolves around the sun every 24 hours. As the Earth spins, distinct parts of it tilt toward the Sun. When the part of Earth where you live is tilted toward the sun, you get longer days and shorter nights (summer). When the part of Earth is tilted away from the Sun, you get shorter days and longer nights (winter). If you lived at the equator you always have day and nights that are 12 hours long.

Day / Light

Light is the form of radiant energy that acts on the retina of the eye and renders objects visible. Light is the absence of darkness or darkness is the total absence of light. The Sun is the major source of light and heat for the Earth. Without the sunlight, Earth would be in perpetual darkness and permanent, eternal frost.

The Sun's output of energy is the same, day to day, month to month, year to year, century to century. This is important because, it means that on any day of the year, at any place on the face of the Earth the amount of sunlight is the same as last year that time. This result in seasons.

It all about Time

In the beginning, indicates the starting point of time and space. This point was the result of an enormous explosion of energy and light that started everything to come into existence: the beginning of the universe, start of space and the start of time (Genesis1:1). Time became official on Earth when the darkness was divided from the light. Time is measured in standard interval of a second, a minute, or an hour. Each day (a twenty-four-hour period) the Earth makes one complete spin or rotation

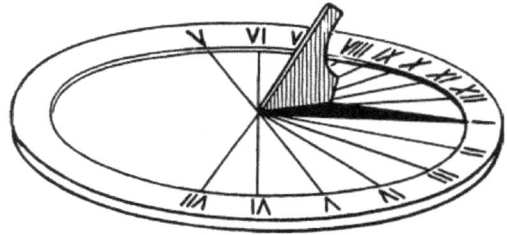

People has always used some sort of method to tell time. Ancients during biblical time used the Sun for timekeeping. For most people, it was 'nighttime' or 'daytime'. One of the earliest devices to measure time was the sundials. A sundial is constructed to show the Sun's motion across the sky revealed on a disk as measurement of shadows. A sundial used in the early Mesopotamia area consists of an upright stick in the ground with time marks around. Later the Egyptians replace the stick with a monument decorated with spires called obelisks, which were place in the city centers for telling the time of the day. The sundial must be aligned with the north-south axis of the Earth. The sundial enabled the Romans to divide the day into 12 equal parts, or hours. Now the whole world's time is synchronized atomic oscillation clock we do not look to the sky for time anymore.

Recording *Time*

The moon completes a revolution around the Earth every 29½ hours which roughly make a month. The Greek used three ten-day weeks per month. The Romans used an eight-day week with the eighth day reserved for market festivities, but after A.D. 200

they changed to a seven-day week. A year consist of the Earth completing a revolution around the Sun of 365 ¼ days. We keep records of seasons and can develop almanac and calendars.

Day Two: Restoration of the Heavens

And God said, "Let there be a firmament in the midst of the waters, and let it divide the waters from the waters. And God made the firmament, and divided the waters which were under the firmament from the waters which were above the firmament: and it was so. And God called the firmament Heaven. And the evening and the morning were the second day" (Genesis 1:6-8).

The firmament (Heb. *shamayin*- expanse, something spread out). The firmament is heaven or the sky above the atmosphere." Can you with Him spread out the sky, which is strong, and as a molten looking glass?" (Job 37:18). God stretches out the north over the empty place and hangs the Earth upon nothing. Earth is suspended in space without any support other than God's power. Science calls this power or force gravity. He (God) sits enthroned above the circle of the earth, and its people are like grasshoppers. He stretches out the heavens like a canopy (thin curtain- atmosphere ozone layer) and spreads them out like a tent to live in. (Isaiah 40:22). The ozone layers protect the Earth from the Sun's harmful ultraviolet radiation and keeps the Earth warm. If the ozone layer, this thin curtain, was removed, life on Earth would die. Harmful rays would burn us, blind us, blister our skin, and kill us. This layer does help to prevent the rapid escape of heat and keep us from freezing. We are also shielded from a constant bombardment of meteors from outer space that burn up before entering our atmosphere.

"But God made the Earth by his power; He founded the world by His wisdom and stretched out the heavens by His understanding. When He uttered His voice, there is a multitude of waters in the heavens, and he causes the vapors to ascend from the ends of the Earth. He makes lightnings with rain, and brings forth the wind out of his treasures" (Jeremiah 10:12-13).

The Atmosphere- the Firmament

The Layers of the Sky

The firmament is called heaven (Hebrews *shamanism* means the heights). The Greek work is *ouranos* that which is raised up or lofty. Heaven is what you see when you stand outside and look up. It is the space which includes the Earth's atmosphere and the celestial realm. In the firmament, we see the Sun, Moon, and Stars. It is also called the expanse or the sky. Scriptures used both tern to refer to three separate places.

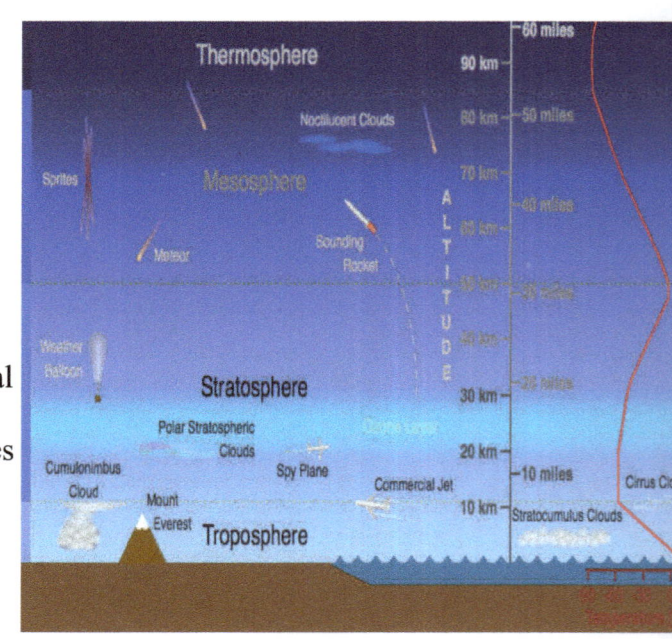

82

First Heaven-Atmospheric Heaven

The atmospheric heaven is the sky or the troposphere. This is the region we call a blanket. The area that contains the breathable region for life. "The windows of heavens were opened. And the rain upon the Earth forty days and forty nights" (Genesis 7:11-12). This heaven is covered with clouds, rain and precipitation are forms there (Deuteronomy 28:12, Acts 14:17); and where the birds fly.

Earth is surrounded by a mixture of gases, solid particles, and liquid vapors called an atmosphere. It is held down or fasten to Earth because of gravity. The main gases in the atmosphere are Nitrogen (78 %) and Oxygen (21%). The remaining percentage of gases include Argon, Carbon dioxide, water vapor, Neon, Helium, methane, Krypton, Hydrogen, and Ozone.

The atmosphere is divided into layers. The layers in order from the closes to the Earth are: **troposphere** (air we breathe, water vapors, and where weather is formed, clouds); **stratosphere** (find the ozone here); **mesosphere** (temperature very low, meteors enter Earth's atmosphere burn up in this layer, find shooting stars); **thermosphere** (temperature rises due to solar radiation) ; **exosphere** (human made satellites orbit here without creating much friction and heat from the movement); and **ionosphere** (layer is composed of ions or electrically charged particles; reflect radio waves for communication).

Fluffy White Clouds

You will find the clouds in the firmament (sky) above the water called the atmosphere. God wraps up the waters in his clouds, yet the clouds do not burst under their weight (Job 26:8). The clouds retain waters and the rain is poured out on the Earth without destroying the clouds by the weight of the water in them. The primary purposes of clouds are to serve as a reservoir of water in vapor form that is available to replenish the Earth's water supply, to cause the bud of tender herbs to spring forth, flourish and nourish the land, to satisfy the desolate and waste ground with water (Job 38:26-29).

There is movement of electricity from cloud to cloud with a light show. The heavens resounded with thunder; your arrows flashed back and forth. (Psalm 77:17). Lightning is like a flashlight in the sky caused by a discharge of electricity between clouds or between one part of a cloud and the Earth. The sound of thunder following the lightning is made by heat from discharge of electricity from the cloud. (Job 38:25).

Clouds are water droplets or ice crystals which have collected on dust or small particles an are suspended in the air. Most clouds form in the troposphere. Condensation happens when the air is saturated and cannot hold any more water vapor. Dew is water in the form of droplets that appears on thin, exposed objects on the Earth surface in the morning or evening due to condensation. As the exposed surface cools by radiating its heat, atmospheric moisture condenses at a rate greater than that at which it can evaporate, resulting in the formation of water droplets. Condensation can occur when the amount of water in the air increases or when the air is cooled to the point of producing dew.

Five factors that influence formation of clouds are: surface heating of the ground by the sun; topography of a region; boundaries between warm air and cool air; air flowing in different directions; and a sudden change in the wind speed of air flow can form clouds. Clouds float because the water droplets that comprise them are so incredibly tiny that they do not fall very fast.

White Clouds in Blue Skies

The water droplets in clouds are large enough that they can scatter through all the wavelengths of the colors of the rainbow: red, orange, yellow, green, blue, indigo and violet. Sunlight scatters more than once when it hits each droplet of the many in each cloud, so by the time the light reaches the human eye, there is no dominance of a specific color. The combination of the seven wavelengths that form the complete color spectrum produces white light, which gives clouds their milky color.

ROY G BIV-red, orange, yellow, green, blue, indigo, violet

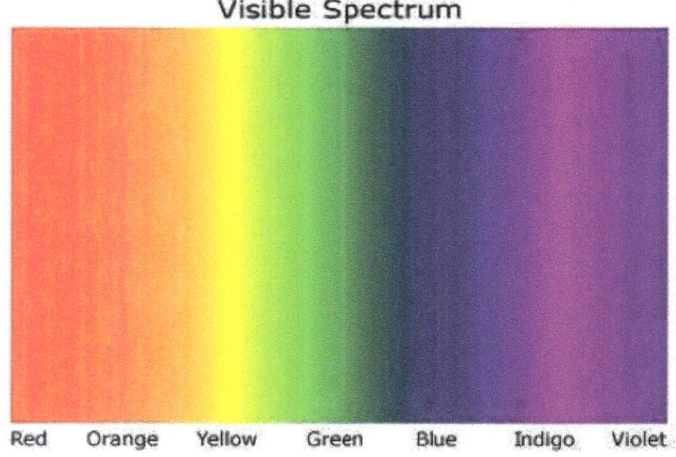

The interactions of sunlight with matter can result in absorption, transmission, and reflection of light waves. The atmosphere is a gaseous sea that contains a variety of types of particles. The two most common types of matter present in the atmosphere are gaseous nitrogen and oxygen. These particles scatter the higher visible light spectrum. This scattering process involves the absorption of a light wave in a variety of directions. Atmospheric nitrogen and oxygen scatter violet light most easily, followed by blue light, green light, etc.

So as white light (ROYGBIV) from the Sun passes through our atmosphere, the high frequencies (BIV) become scattered by atmospheric particles while the lower frequencies (ROY) are most likely to pass through the atmosphere without a significant alteration in their direction. This scattering of the higher frequencies of light illuminates the skies with light on the BIV end of the visible spectrum. Compared to blue light, violet light is most easily scattered by atmospheric particles. However, our eyes are more sensitive to light with blue frequencies. Thus, we view the skies as being blue in color.

Types of Clouds

Clouds can be classified by their shapes: stratus, cumulus, cirrus. Stratus clouds are layered clouds and cover the sky. They can be close to the ground and create a fog and produce light drizzle. Cumulus clouds are thick and puffy like cotton balls. They indicate that fair weather is ahead and form on warm days. Cirrus clouds are light and feather-like. They indicate fair-weather or a weather change. They are made of chilly water or ice crystals in high in the air.

Clouds are natural occurrence in the sky used by God for shelter, protection, and guidance

1. Adam and Eve lived in the garden of Eden and a mist water the garden. A mist brings vapors, warm and humid atmosphere. It waters the face of the ground(Earth). It is like a fog that dissipate when the Sun is out. Fogs are a type of low lying clouds near the surface of the Earth. It is heavily influenced by nearby bodies of water, wind conditions, and topography. In the morning, it would condense to dew on the ground and plants. (Genesis 2:6; Songs of Solomon 2:4)

2. God put a rainbow in the clouds to serve as a covenant. A reminder of a promise made to mankind and all creation. "Whenever I bring clouds over the earth and the rainbow appears in the clouds, I will remember my covenant between me and you and all living creatures of every kind. Never again will the waters become a flood to destroy all life" (Genesis 9:13-16; Ezekiel 1:28; Revelations 10:1)).

3. A little cloud rising out of the sea like a man's hand was an act of restoring rain after a drought (1 Kings 18:44-45; Zechariah 10:1).

4. Clouds are the amazing works of God (Psalm 77;17-19; Job 22:13-14; Job 37:9-11)

5. Part of the water cycle-rain is produced from vapors ascending to cold air, becoming condensed into water that falls again in the form of rain. (Ecclesiastes 11:3; Genesis 2:6).

6. Serve as shade or shelter from the heat of the sun. The clouds provided a shadow (Isaiah 25:5).

7. Clouds have speed and mobility (Isaiah 60:8).

8. Withholding of rain from the clouds (Leviticus 26:19; Isaiah 5:6))

9. Sign of God's presence as a pillar of cloud (Exodus 13:21-22; Exodus 40:38; Numbers 10:34).

10. Clouds and forecast weather," Mankind can see a cloud rising in the west and predict a shower is coming and no ability to interpret the conditions of the present time" (Luke 12:54).

11. As Israel left Egypt and were roaming in the wilderness to Canaan clouds were a signal for movement and breaking up or setting camp (Exodus 40:36-38).

12. Symbols of pride of wicked (Job 20:6)
13. Cloud illumination as a pillar of fire by night (Psalm 105:39; Exodus 14:20)
14. Jesus returning to Earth on a cloud with power and glory (Matthew 24:30; Luke 12:54; Mark 13:26).

Planetary Heaven-Second Heaven

The second heaven is where the stars, the moon, and the planets are located. It is outer space. And God," Let there be lights in the firmament of the heaven to divide the day from the night" (Genesis 1:14-17). The heaven declares the glory of God; the skies proclaim the work of his hands. Day after day they pour forth speech; night after night they reveal knowledge. They have no speech, they use no words; no sound is heard from them. In heavens God has pitched a tent for the Sun. It is like a bridegroom coming our o his chamber, and rejoicing as a strong man run his race. It rises at one end of the heavens and makes its circuit to the other and nothing stops it heat" (Psalm 19:1-6). Both the Earth and the Sun travel eternally in their own circuits and orbits. The Sun moves through space at the rate of 43,200 mph. The surface temperature of the Sun is about 12000 °F and about 40,000,000 °F at the center. The extreme heat makes it impossible for life as we know it to exist on the Sun.

When King Nebuchadnezzar destroyed Jerusalem, the Babylonians ransack the graves of kings, princes, and other loved one for their bones to spread before the Sun, Moon, and the Planets which they had worshipped (Jeremiah 8:2). The Stars are also located in the second heaven. "For the Stars of heaven and the constellations shall not give light, and the sun shall be darkened, and the moon shall not shine during the judgment in the Day of the Lord" (Isaiah 13:10).

Third Heaven

This is the habitation of God," Our Father who art in haven, hallowed be your name (Matthew 5:9); Jesus on the right hand making intercessions on our behalf (Hebrew 9:24); Brothers and Sister in Christ have citizenship (Philippians 3:23) and His holy angels are present around the throne of God (Job 1:6). When Solomon dedicated the temple, his prayer included a reference to the dwelling place of God, "Behold, the heaven and heaven of heavens (or the highest of heavens) cannot contain thee; how much less this house that I have built?" (1 Kings 8:27). "Behold the heaven and the heaven of heavens is the LORD'S your God, the Earth also, with all that is within it belongs to Him "(Deuteronomy 10:14).

Nevertheless, God is omnipresent. God is everywhere. His dwelling place, haven, is not subject to the normal limitation of human that live in finite dimensions." Where can I go from your Spirit? Where can I flee from your presence? If I go up to heavens, you are there; if I make my bed in the depths you are there If I rise on the wings of the dawn, if I settle on the far side of the sea, even there your hand will guide me, your right hand will hold me fast. If I say, "Surely the darkness will hide me and the light become night around me," even the darkness will not be dark to you; the night will shine like the day, for darkness is as light to you" (Psalm 139: 1-12)

Day Three-Restoration of the Seas and the Land

"And God called the dry land ground; and the gathering together of the waters He called the Seas: and God saw that it was good" (Genesis 1:10).

> Water, Water, Water everywhere- water under the Earth, in the Earth, on the Earth and above the Earth

Earth is the only known planet with liquid water on its surface. The seas in scripture refers to a gathering of the waters. The waters were contained in basins. These basins or beds formed oceans, rivers, lakes, seas that could connect to each other. An ocean is a large body of body of salt water. The great body of waters that embrace large land masses are continents Scientist believe that at one time, a supercontinent called Pangaea existed. Scientist believe the supercontinent broke up into two continents called Gondwanaland and Laurasia. Over time the continent began to drift apart. "In the days of Peleg, the Earth divided" (Genesis 10:25). A geophysicist by the name of Alfred Wegener was the scientist who proposed the Continental Drift Theory in the early twentieth century.

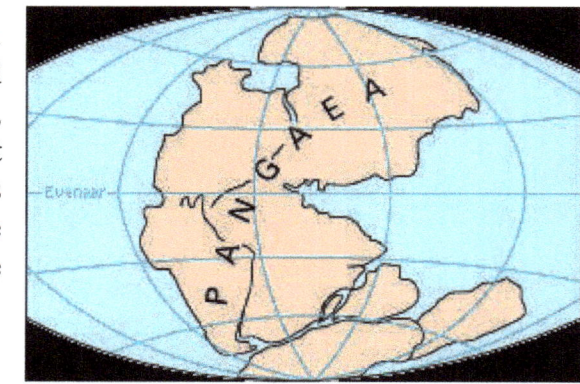

The present days oceans are the Pacific, the Atlantic, the Indian, Antarctic and the Arctic oceans.

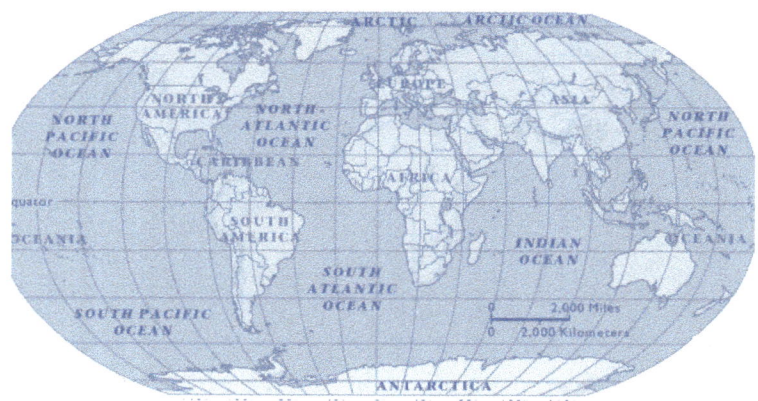

The continents today are North America, South America, Antarctica, Africa, Australia, India, and Eurasia. Seventy percent of the Earth's surface is covered with oceans. About two-thirds of the Earth's land area is found in the Northern Hemisphere, which is only 61% ocean. About 89% of the Southern Hemisphere is ocean. The ocean is about 3.5% salt. Salts and minerals are dissolved in the ocean like a big solution.

The main difference between salt water and fresh water is the salinity content. Both contain salt. The Earth's oceans and seas are saltwater system. While the lakes, river, streams, marshes and ponds are fresh water system.

The Pacific Ocean is the world's largest and deepest ocean. The Arctic Ocean is the smallest and shallowest oceans. We also have seas, such as the Mediterranean Sea, the Gulf Mexico, and the South China Sea. These large bodies of water affect the climate on land through ocean breezes, storms (tsunami, hurricanes, typhoons-Acts 27:9-14), conduction of heat, winds, water cycle (Isaiah 55:8-11; Jeremiah 10:13; Psalm 135:7), Ecclesiastic 11:3), cycling nutrients (magnesium, calcium, potassium, sulfate), replenish atmospheric oxygen, and the changes in weather (Psalm 107:25).

Oceans provide 90% of the Earth's living space. Ninety-seven percent of the planet's water is contained in the oceans. The longest continuous mountain chain in the known universe is underwater. Ocean water never stops moving. There are three basic motions of ocean water: the up and down movement of waves, the steady movement of ocean currents, and the rise and fall of ocean water in tides. Waves are pulses of energy that move through the ocean.

Gravity pulls all matter towards the center of the Earth. This keeps the water in lower basin called seas and ocean and is bounded by higher ground called continents and islands.

God established forces and boundaries to stop the strong waves of the oceans. They advance as if nothing could stop them, but when they come to God's established boundaries they are broken and stopped at the shore. The world's ocean contains nearly 30 million tons of Gold.

Ocean waves are caused by wind moving across the surface of the water. The friction between the air molecules and the water molecules causes energy to be transferred from the wind to the water. This causes waves to form." *Ducksters.com Earth Science, Ocean Waves and Currents*

The Earth remain safe if the seas remain in its place. (Job 38:8-11). Where the land meets the sea is the coast. The coast can be rock, sandy, muddy, or marshy.

"Adam and Eve had a water system in the Garden of Eden. A river flows out of Eden to water the garden and from there divides into four rivers. The first is named Pishon; it flows through Havilah where there is gold. The gold of this land is good aromatic resin and onyx. The second river is named Gihon; it flows through the land of Cush. The third river is named Hiddekel (Tigris) it runs along the east side of Asshur (Assyria). The fourth river is the Euphrates" (Genesis 2:10-14)

God speaks to us through nature and used water to miraculously rescue the Israelites. If the oceans dry up the life forms on Earth would cease to exist.

Important Properties of Water

Spiritual Application of Water	Natural Application of Water
Purification from sin (Numbers 8:7, 31:23)	Life on Earth began in water
Spirit baptism or enduement of power from on high (Luke 24:49, John 7:37-39, Acts 1:4-5)	All living organisms require water more than any other substance
Daily supply (Psalm 23:2)	Water has cohesive property. They stay close together due to their hydrogen bonds. Plants can transport water from root up to the leaves into the veins and back down to the roots
Spiritual growth (Psalm 1:3)	Water is less dense as a sold than as a liquid. This is how ice floats in liquid water. Water expands when frozen not contract like most substances.
Instability (Genesis 49:4)	Water dissolved more solute than any liquid It is called the universal solvent.
Word of God (John 3:5; Ephesian 5:26; James 1:18)	Large bodies of water can absorb and store a huge amount of heat energy from the Sun during the daytime. This heat is release during the night and create a cool breeze over land.
Baptism as a symbol of the death, burial, and resurrection of Jesus Christ (1 Peter 3:21)	Water acts as an insulation for aquatic life below a frozen layer.
In times of troubles (Psalm 69:1-2; Isaiah 48:1)	Water has a high surface tension that result from the strength of its hydrogen bonds and allow small insects to water on the surface of a pond.
Blessings will be return to you (Ecclesiastes 11:1)	Water also influence weather. Water molecules regulate air temperature by absorbing heat from the air that is warmer and releasing heat to air that is cooler.

Meteorological Phenomena- Effects of water on the Earth's surface(land) and Atmosphere

Another consideration for the continental separation could be explained through Noah's flood experience. Flooding happen after extreme heavy rainfall. Flooding is an overflowing of water onto land that is normally dry. They can occur quickly or over long periods of time and can last from a day, to weeks, or longer. Flood are considered natural disasters.

The Hebrew term for heavy rain is *geshem* which means violent rains (Ezekiel 13:11-13) .

Noah lived during a time when humans had every inclination of wicked thoughts, evil in their hearts, and were full of violence. Noah was a righteous man. This does not mean that Noah was perfect but was faithful to God compared to his contemporaries (Genesis 6:1-11). God told Noah to build an ark and that He is going to bring flood waters on the Earth that will result in the destruction of all life under the heaven (Genesis 6:17). This type of flood was probably a flash flood.

Floods are the result of *meteorological* (relates to the atmosphere and forecasting the weather), *hydrological* (properties of water and it relationship to the movement of land) and *geological* (the Earth physical substance and structures) conditions together. The possibility of flooding taking place might include the following factors: how hard the rain falls, how fast it is raining; how long it is raining; how porous the soil; amount of vegetation; how wide an area getting rain; and geography and slope of the land.

Flash floods are the most dangerous kinds of floods. They combine destructive power of a flood with incredible speed and unpredictability. They can happen with little or no warning. The Bible declares the people were given 120 years warning before the rain started (Genesis 6:3,17). A little less than seventy-four years out of the 120 years Noah was building an Ark as instructed by God. When Noah finished building, and filling the Ark, God told Noah and his family (only seven people) now is the time to enter the ark (Genesis 7:1). Noah was six hundred years old when the floodwater came to the Earth (Genesis 7:6). "And after the seven days of entering the ark, the floodwaters came to the Earth" (Genesis 7:10).

Start of the Longest Rain Recorded in the Bible

Aside from Noah's flood in the Bible, the largest floods were the 1931 central China floods, which occurred from July to August and affected the Yellow, Yangtze, and Huai Rivers. The human casualties are estimated from 3.7 million to 4 million.

In the six hundredth year and on the seventeenth day of the second month of Noah's life he could have written the following: On this day all the springs of the great deep burst forth and the floodgates of the heavens were opened. The rain fell on the Earth forty days and forty nights" (Genesis 7:11-13). This is what could have possibly taken place in the mountains and steep hills producing rapid runoff, which caused streams to rise quickly. Rocks and clay solids could have prevented the water from infiltrating the ground. Saturated soil can lead to rapidly increase of flooding. Higher than average tides might have occurred and onshore winds result from low atmosphere pressure. For the flood to take hold so fast on the land the question is, "How quick can the land be covered by water?" NOAA (National Oceanic and Atmospheric Administration) stated, "If thunderstorms linger for extended periods of time over the area of a creek six inches deep in the mountain, it can swell into a ten-foot-deep raging river in less than an hour. "

"The waters rose and covered the mountains to a depth of more than fifteen cubits (about 23 feet)" (Genesis 7:19-20). The water was deep enough to keep the ark floating and not running aground. After a period, God sent a wind (Heb. *rachaph*) over the Earth (Genesis 8:1). In Genesis 1:2 this wind is called the Spirit of God. Energy is always needed to bring about changes. The water started to recede from the land and the occupants of the Ark were given permission to leave on dry land (Genesis (8:6-18).

Table: Global Flooding of the Earth (Land)
Duration of Noah inside the Ark was 377 Days (12 months and 17 days)

Event	Days	Scriptures	What was happening to the Land?
Approx. 74 years			Noah builds the Ark
1 week getting settled in the Ark	1	Genesis 7:1-10	God orders Noah to enter the Ark and the flood begins
40 days and 40 nights	40	Genesis 7:11	Flood starts-fountains of the great deep were burst open, the windows of the heaven were opened
On the 40th day of the flood		Genesis 7:18	Ark is lifted off the ground and floats. Rain continued to fall past this date and increased greatly
The fountains of the deep and the windows of the heavens were closed	150	Genesis 7:24-8:4 The rain was restrained - Genesis 8:2	Rain stops and Ark rests on Mountains of Ararat. The water would now begin to decrease
	224	Genesis 8:5	Mountains visible. Noah could begin to see the tops of the hills rising above the waters. This is 74 days after the ark rested on the mountain side.
	264	Genesis 8:6-7	Raven sent out to scout the land, but would flying back and forth for the next 107 days until the land was completely dry.
Dove sent out the first time	271	Genesis 8: 8-9	Dove sent out as a scout but sufficient dry land was not found, so it returned to Noah's ark
Dove sent out the second time	278	Genesis 8:10-11	The dove was sent back out and came back this time with a freshly plucked olive leaf. Noah now knew the water had subsided
Dove sent out the third time	285	Genesis 8:12	Flood over. This time the dove found sufficient dry land for its and did not return to the ark
Most of the waters dried from the land	314	Genesis 8:13	Noah open the door to the ark. The water had mostly dried from the ground, but there was still water that had not soaked in, and Noah could not exit at this time.
Land dried	371	Genesis 8:14	Noah and family leaves the ark

Shaking and Quaking from Fault Lines

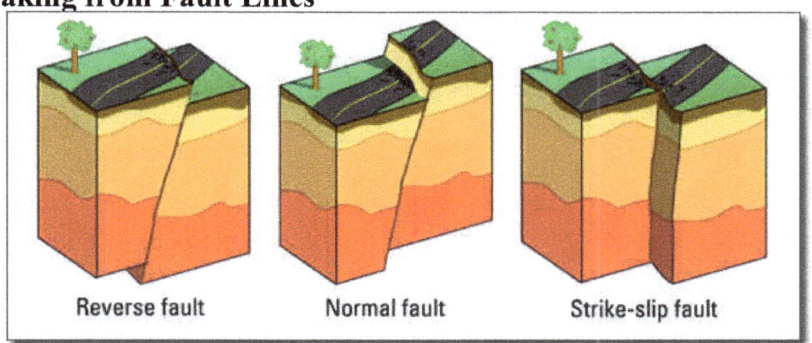

They are those that doubt that the flood was universal. Let us keep in mind that the Earth was one vast block of land and was not divided into continents and islands until possibly after the flood as mentioned in Genesis 10:25. Also, some believe that the continental separation might have occurred during the Towel of Babel incident of all the people of the Earth scattered (Genesis 11). The reasoning behind the last statement is if this was the case another global flood would have had to happen or this was a miracle of moving the people far way on floating land masses.

This flood could be described in tectonic terms as "all the fountains of the great deep broken up and the flood gates open" called subterranean water (Genesis 7:11-12, Psalm 18:5. Job 38:8-11, Proverbs 3:20). Subterranean waters or subsurface waters run wholly or partly beneath the ground surface. It is located in rocks in the upper portion of the Earth's crust in a liquid, solid, or gaseous state. The Hebrew word for "broken up" is *baga* and is used to refer to a geological phenomenon called faults in a plate. A fault is a break in the rocks that make up the Earth's crust along which rocks on either side have moved past each other. An example of this breaking up of the ground was when Moses and Israelites were in the wilderness. "As soon as he (Moses) finished speaking to the congregation, the ground under them split apart and the Earth opened its mouth and swallowed the protesters, their possessions, and their household" (Numbers 16:31).

The flood water may have triggered the earth crust and fragmented into plates releasing subterranean water, volcanic gas, and lava. The mountains became visible from the ark on the day 223 (Genesis 8:5). The retreat of the flood water can be connected to plate tectonics. "The mountains rose up; the valleys sank down, springs poured back into the ravines" (Psalm 104:6-8). They were many catastrophic forces during Noah's flood which could break up the lithosphere plates.

God gave humankind a promise never to flood the complete Earth ever again.

Faults Lines

The lithosphere is the brittle but slightly elastic layer of the solid Earth. The tectonic plates are segment of the lithosphere. Mountains of Ararat is the traditional resting place of Noah's ark. It is in eastern Turkey near the Armenian and Iranian borders (Genesis 8:3-4). Turkey is one of the world's more active earthquake and volcanic region. The Ark rested on the Mountains of Ararat for 2 1/2 months before the tops of the mountain range were visible. The Mountains of Ararat is a tectonically active region at the junction of three lithospheric plates. There is academic support for the proposal that separation of the continents, rifting of the ocean floor, under thrusting of ocean trenches were accomplished by rapid processes not occurring today. This could have been accomplished by Noah's flood.

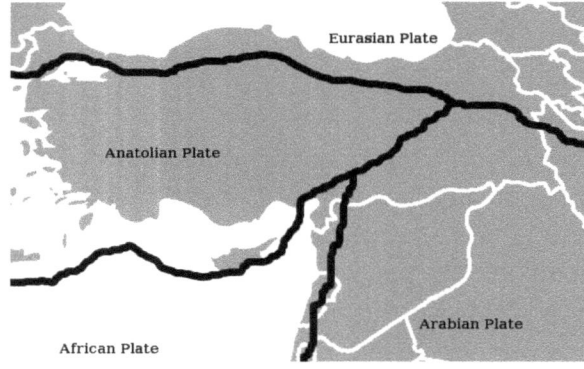

Claims to the "Promised Land"

Land is not easy to destroy. The Law of the Conservation of Energy is that "Energy cannot be created or destroyed but transformed or transferred to another form. As a result, the original energy God put in creation of all things is in a closed system that cannot change even after volcanic activities and the dropping of the Atom Bomb. The land had natural powers to restore itself over time. Land can be grades in difference quality- barren, fertile, dry, dusty, poor, and sandy. Land cannot be moved bodily from one place to another without a vast energy input that can cause the Earth to shake and roll like in earthquakes. However, mud, sludge, ooze (soft, sticky matter resulting from the mixing of earth and water) can slide when affected by the following factors: gravity, weather, groundwater, wave action, geology, and human actions.

Land can be altered for different uses like building roads. The atmosphere and oceans of the Earth continuously shape the land by eroding and transporting solids on the surface. Lastly, land is not man-made (Genesis 1:1).

Genesis reveals the life of one family and their connection to the land. Land was very important to the Patriarchs. All life and survival were linked to the land. Everything that they used can be traced back to the land. Land was the source of material wealth and economic prosperity of a country. Transportation throughout the country was depended upon the topography of the land.

The family story opens with God formed Adam out of the fertile ground (land) and breathed (puffed) life into his nostril (Genesis 2:7). God made a garden from very fertile land. This garden was East of Eden. Out of the ground grew every tree and plant. In the very center stood the Tree of Life and the Tree of Knowledge. Adam and Eve were given the responsibility to take care of the land and animals (Genesis 2:8-9). Adam and Eve disobeyed a command of God. This resulted in them being expelled from the fertile land of the garden of Eden. At the east of Eden, God stationed cherubim and placed a flaming sword to guard the entrance to the Garden and to the Tree of Life. Because they ate of the Tree of Knowledge of good and evil, the ground was cursed in that, it would be hard to cultivate with weeds and dried soil. Thorns (used as crown on Christ's head- Matthew 27:29, Psalm 24:31) and thistles (weeds) would come forth from the ground, and Adam and Eve and the family to follow would labor hard and farm land the for herbs, vegetation, and fruits to eat.

Centuries had passed since the flood and now we see the generation after Noah settling in the plains of Shinar (Babylonia). The people of Babel built a tower (Ziggurats) out of bricks. The tower was built out of mud bricks. Mud and straw are mixed together, shaped in wooden molds, then left to dry in the sun. Then the bricks were laid with tar for mortar. The people had one language but God scrabble their language and scattered them across the face of all the Earth (the land). All this technology was developed from products of the land (Genesis 11:1-8).

Abram and his family led a nomadic life. They traveled from place to place looking for grazing land and water. They carried all their possession on camels and lived in tents. The Lord made a covenant with Abram saying, "Unto thy seed (offspring) have I given this land (Canaan) from the River of Egypt unto the River Euphrates" (Genesis 15:18).

Joseph family went to live in Egypt to escape from famine in their own country, they were given land in Goshen, in the north of the country. Because there was plenty of water there, the Israelites grew many crops. Upon Joseph's death, he requested that his embalmed body be taken to the land that was sworn to Abraham, to Isaac, and to Jacob, the Promised Land. (Genesis 50:24).

The Promised Land was a land described as a good spacious land; as flowing with milk and honey. The plains and hills were good land for farmers who grew crops of wheat, barley, groves of olives and fig trees, and vineyards (Exodus 3:8). But, the land was occupied by the Canaanites, Hittites, Amorites, Perizzites, Hivites, Amorites, and the Jebusites (Exodus 3:8). There will be a big fight for the land.

Surveying the Landforms

Landforms are the features on the surface of the Earth. They can be mountains (land that rises above the surrounding area), plains (a large grassy flat areas), and plateau (a high, flat landform with steep sides). You will also find canyons, beaches and valleys.

Landforms are the features or characteristics of a given landscape.

1. **Mountain** – any area of land that rises above the surrounding area. Mountains are formed when two of the continental plates that make up the Earth's crust collides. The force caused by the collision pushes both plates (also called tectonic plates) upward, creating a mountain. Mountains have been formed by volcanic eruptions, earthquakes, and other strong forces. Mountains trembled at God's awesome presence (Judges 5:5; Habakkuk 3:3-6). On Mt. Sinai God gave Moses the Law -Ten Commandments (Exodus 24:12).

2. **Plain** – a large flat area. It is a largely grassy area with slow-moving streams. Coastal plains are found near the shore, and inland plains are found in the landlocked interior of the continent. Serve as a camping ground (Numbers 22:1, Joshua 4:13, Judges 1:19); Chariots travel (Jeremiah 52:8).

3. **Plateau**- is a raised, relatively level area that is higher than the land on at least one side of it. If a river runs through a plateau, it tends to make a deep gorge. Location of township (Deuteronomy 3:10, Joshua 13:9, Jeremiah 21:13).

4. **Valley**- is a low-lying area of land that is usually found at the foot of mountains or hills. The most common valleys are formed by erosion of land from running water. Valleys and caves are natural features created by erosion and the movement of the Earth's crust. Battle ground, worship place, and pastures for crops (Genesis 14:8, 2 Chronicles 28:3, Psalm 65:13, Psalm 23:12.

5. **Canyon**- a deep valley with cliffs on both sides (Gen 26:17, Numbers 13:23, Deuteronomy 3:8).

6. **Caves-**are huge holes under the ground, in cliffs or under the sea. Caves can be formed by rainwater that seeps into tiny cracks in the rocks. The rainwater contains minerals and chemicals that slowly causes the rock to dissolve, leaving behind a large hole. Serves as shelter, a hiding place, a home (Judges 6:2, 2 Samuel 13:6, 1 Kings 18:4, Hebrew 11:38).

7. **Rift valley-** created when two tectonic plates pull away from each other, leaving low space in the middle. The soil covering the plates fell and forms a rift valley (Genesis 7:11).

8. **Islands-** a piece of land surrounded by water (Isaiah 11:11, Acts 27:16, Acts 28:9).

Colonization of the Land

"And God said, Let the earth bring forth grass, the herb yielding seed, and the fruit tree yielding fruit after his kind, whose seed is, upon the earth: and it was so· And the earth brought forth grass, and herb yielding seed after his kind, and the tree yielding fruit, whose seed was, after his kind: and God saw that it was good. And the evening and the morning were the third day" (Genesis 1:11-13).

The air, water, and land were now restored and in perfect conditions to bring forth a diversity of plants. This diverse group included three distinct kinds of vegetation (Heb. *deshe`*): grass, the herbs, and the trees. These plants were photosynthetic plants. Photosynthetic plants were organisms that captured radiant energy from the Sun and produce organic compounds like glucose and released oxygen gas to the atmosphere.

Importance of Plants

Plants are important to the balance of nature. Plants play many important roles in the environment. Primarily plants provide us with food and useful products. They are important to the balance of nature by recycling elements from fallen decaying leaven that replenish the soil with natural fertilizers. Plants play another key role in the environment by renewing the atmosphere with oxygen and absorbing carbon dioxide. Probably bacteria, microbes, and fungi were formed in this synthesis of raw materials. The Bible does not use the terms microbes, germ, or viruses but they did exist.

Plants regulate the water cycle: they help distribute and purify the planet's water. They also help move water from the soil to the atmosphere through a process called transpiration. Transpiration is the process by which moisture is carried through plants from roots to small pores on the underside of leaves, where it changes to vapor and is released to the atmosphere. Transpiration is essentially evaporation of water from plant leaves. Animals use plants for shelter and many medicines are derived from plants. Plants also help to regulate the climate by removing some of the carbon in the atmosphere to reduce the greenhouse effect.

Natural patterns or cycles were established during creation that would not change. While the earth remains, seedtime and harvest, and cold and heat, and summer and winter, and day and night shall not cease (Genesis 8:22). God proclaimed His laws of nature that were unfailing and unchangeable and would be enforced as long as Earth exist (Be not deceived; God is not mocked: for whatsoever a man soweth, that shall he also reap" (Galatians 6:7).

God's ordinances or natural laws still in existence are:

- Seedtime and harvest – The law can be stated as "If you sow you will reap".
- Pattern of seasons will affect the plant's life – Summer and Winter

- Temperature influences the plant cycle – cold and heat
- Day and Night- radiant energy affect the rate of photosynthesis
- Environment and habitat best suited for growth

Plant diversity – History of the Plant Kingdom

The early plant like algae that were formed in the water and was followed by seedless, nonvascular plants (lack conducts tubes or tissues for transport of water) called bryophytes. Bryophytes includes mosses, liverworts, and hornworts. They lack true roots and leaves and do not good have upright support and cover the land like carpet, require moister conditions for fertilization and disperse their offspring as spores carried by the air.

The next group of plants involves those that provide strong support, with stems to stand upright and grow tall on land and are called vascular plants. Vascular plants are made up of ducts or vessels (xylem and phloem) that conduct water, sap, food through the plant and provide mechanical support.

Vascular plants can be grouped as seedless vascular spores (ferns, horsetails clubmosses) and seed plants. Having reproductive components that are sperm producing (pollen) and egg producing parts of the plant. The flower is the center of reproduction for this type of plant.

Seeds

Plants were also commanded by God to reproduce after its own kind. (Genesis 1:11) The reproductive unit of a flowering plant is the seed. The miracle of the seed is the number of fruits or other plant parts that will be produce from the germination of one seed.

A seed is a mature fertilized ovule of angiosperms and gymnosperms that contains an embryo and the food it will need to grow into a new plant. The seeds of gymnosperms (such as the conifers) develop on scales of cones or similar structures, while the seeds of angiosperms are enclosed in an ovary that develops into a fruit, such as a pome or nut. The structure of seeds varies somewhat. All seeds are enclosed in a protective seed coat.

Seeds can be carried by wind, air, or animals to new locations from the original plant. After the seeds has made it to a new location and is covered with dirt, it can begin germination.

Germination is the process of seeds developing into new plants. First, environmental conditions must trigger the seed to grow. Usually, this is determined by how deep the seed is planted, water availability, and temperature. When water is plentiful, the seed fills with water in a process called imbibition. The water activates special proteins, called enzymes, that begin the process of seed growth. First the seed grows a root to access water underground. Next, the shoots, or growth above ground, begin to appear. The seed sends a shoot towards the surface, where it will grow leaves to harvest energy from the Sun. The leaves continue to grow towards the light source.

Green, flowering plants have six parts: stem, root, leaf, flower, fruit, and seeds. Angiosperms (Greek. *angion*-container; Greek. *sperma* –seed) are flowering plants. The Angiosperms are seed bearing plants whose seeds are contained in an ovary inside a fruit. The leaves of the angiosperms are flat. They are divided into two categories: monocotyledons and dicotyledons.

Angiosperms

Monocots flower petals usually occur in multiples of 3's. They have parallel veins, spreading roots, and one cotyledon in the seed. Cotyledon is the embryo leaf inside the seed.

Dicots flower petals can be counted in multiples of four or five. They have net veins, taps roots, two cotyledons in the seed.

Gymnosperms (Greek. *gymnos* – naked seed) are those whose seeds are exposed and not enclosed in an ovule. The gymnosperms are cone bearing or needle-like leaves. The gymnosperms are known as softwood as they can last during the winter while. They are conifers (cone-bearing trees) like Pine, Spruce, and Fir.

Herbs

Herbs have been used mostly for their culinary and medical benefits. Herbs are any plants used for food, flavoring, medicine, or fragrances for their savory or aromatic properties. Herbs refers to the leafy green or flowering parts of a plant. Herbs in the Bible are aloes, anise, balm, cinnamon, cumin, garlic, frankincense, mint, mustard, myrrh, saffron and bitter herbs. (Proverbs 5:4; Luke 11:42; Exodus 12:22; Matthew 2:11).

Grasses

Grasses are vegetation consisting of typically short plants with long narrow leaves, growing wild or cultivated on lawns and pasture, and as a fodder crop. They are mainly herbaceous (soft stemmed plants) plant which has jointed stems and spikes of small, wind- pollinated flowers.

Examples of grasses in scripture are barley, flax, wheat, leek, onion, oats, rye, and clover. (Exodus 2:3; Matthew 27:29; John 6:9; Ruth 2:14; Isaiah 47:14).

Flowering Plants

A flower or a blossom is the reproductive structure found in plants. The biological function of a flower is to aid in reproduction by providing a mechanism for the union of sperm with eggs. Flowers may cross pollinate or self- pollinate. Many flowers are attractive to animals that help to transfer of pollen. After fertilization, the ovary of the flower develops into fruit containing seeds. The three most popular flowers in the Bible are lily, rose, and camphire. (Song of Solomon 2:1; Luke 12:27; Matthew 6:8)

Fruit production

Flowers role in the ecosystem is to produce seeds and fruits inside the flower. Bees, butterflies, other insects, and birds help flowers reproduce by carrying pollen from one flower to another. This process is called pollination. The pollen grains travel down through the style into the ovary of the flower. The pollen grain fertilizes the eggs cells in the ovules, and seeds begin to form. As the seeds grown the ovary walls grow into the fruit that will house the seeds. Fruits develop in many various locations. Examples of fruits are pomegranates, dates, figs, grapes, olives, apricot/apple).

Fruits have a vital role in keeping life during biblical time. (Deuteronomy 8:7-8; Numbers 11:5, 2 Samue16:1).
Fruits can grow in a variety of place, "On the high mountain of Israel, I will plant it, that it may bring forth boughs and bear fruit and become a stately cedar. And birds of every kind will nest under it; they will nest in the shade of its branches" (Ezekiel 17:23). For fruit to produce they must be connected to the tree. "Abide in Me, and I in you. As the branch cannot bear fruit of itself unless it abides in the vine, so neither can you unless you abide in Me" (John 15:4-5). You can identify a specific tree by the fruit it. "Either make the tree good and its fruit will be good, or make the tree bad and its fruit will be bad: for the tree is known by its fruit.
Plants need water and soil for anchorage. "He will be like a tree firmly planted by streams of water. Which yields its fruit in its season and its leaf does not wither" (Psalm1:3). Fruits can be dried for preservation for future use - raisin cakes (Hosea 3:1-). Fruits can group in different arrangements like a cluster. (Numbers 13:23-24-clusters of grapes). Fruits can be used to name a person, name cities and towns, used for decoration, and used to dye textiles.

Evidence of the Holy Spirit influencing your life is the effect the spirit has on you. Fruits are used as a symbol of a good spiritual life. Even Spirit yield fruits in a spiritual good life. But the fruit of the Spirit is love(compassionate), joy (gladness), peace (repose, harmony), patience (longsuffering), kindness (gentleness, benevolent), goodness (virtuous), faithfulness (wholehearted confidence), gentleness (meekness, even balance) and self-control (temperance)" (Galatians 5:22-23).

Fruit bearing Trees

Trees play a crucial role in our lives like other green plants. They provide shelter (Exodus 37:1-5), filter and clean the air, regulate climate and distribute raw materials. Trees cover at least 27% of the land. They are called groves if they grow in small groups and forest when many in number over large areas.

Tree tend to live for prolonged period. They can reach up to hundreds of years and beyond. The oldest currently living tree is in White Mountains, California and is 5,066 years old. A plant must reach a minimum height of 9- 19 feet to be classified as a tree. The tallest tree is a giant coastal redwood that is 116 meters tall. The major tree organs consist of a woody trunk, roots, leaves, and branches.

The scriptures warn us against harming fruit trees. "When you besiege a city a long time, to make war against it to capture it, you shall not destroy its trees by swinging an axe against them; for you may eat from them, and you shall not cut them down. For is the tree of the field a man, that it should be besieged by you? Only the trees which you know are not fruit trees you shall destroy and cut down, that you may construct siege works against the city that is making war with you until it falls" (Deuteronomy 20:20-21).

Tree portraits miraculous powers. "And the LORD God planted a garden eastward in Eden; and there he put Adam and Eve, whom he had formed. And out of the ground the LORD God caused to grow every tree that is pleasing to the sight and good for food; the Tree of life also in the midst of the garden, and the Tree of the knowledge of good and evil". Most food is eaten because it is good to the eyes as well as taste. The Tree of Life would give life eternally. (Genesis 3:1-2)" (Genesis 2:8-9).

Examples of Trees in the Bible are poplar, willow, cedar, oak, pine, and cypress (Ezekiel 17:5; Hosea 4:13; Ecclesiasticus 24:14; Genesis 30:37; 2 Samuel 5:11). Foreign trees brought back for rare timbers such as Algum wood (1 Kings 10:10-11; 2 Chronicles 2:8).
Water, soil, sunlight, and micronutrients are needed for the growth of trees to yield fruits. The Bible reveals a miracle of the budding of Aaron's rod. Miracle show us how God can and will do the impossible. While the Israelites were wandering in the wilderness and undergoing all types of trails for survival they began to question the leadership of Moses and Aaron. They grumbled and complained so much that many formed rebellious groups. Later they were judged for their actions by God and loss their life and plagues followed. God had a plan to help show the people who and how He would affirm the person for leadership as High Priest.

Bare Rod -- Sprouted-- Budded-- Blossomed -- Produced Fruit Overnight

Tell the people of Israel to bring you twelve wooden staffs or rods from each leader of each tribes. Each leader is to inscribe

their name on his rod. A rod was possibly a dead limb off a tree; a broken branch off a treed, or a dead stick or staff. Moses was told to inscribe Aaron's name on the staff for the tribe of the Levi. Buds will sprout on the rod belonging to the man I will choose.

When Moses went into the Tabernacle of the Covenant the next day, he found that Aaron's rod, had sprouted, budded, blossomed, and produced ripe almonds.
(Numbers 17:1-12). Flowers came from a dead piece of wood and God caused almonds to grow on it. The almond tree needs hundreds of hours below 45 degrees Fahrenheit to break the dormancy of a bud. The almond flowers are white to pale pink with five petals and appear before the leaves in early Spring. The trees reach full bearing five to six years after planting and fruit matures in about 7-8 months after flowering. It is no less a miracle of an unattached branch completing the entire life cycle overnight.

105

Poplar Trees

Branches, Twigs, Leaves, Needles and Winds :Nature Orchestra

"When you hear a sound like marching feet in the tops fo the popular trees, be on the alert! That will be the signal that the Lord is moving ahead of you to strike down the Philistine army" 2 Samuel 5:24

The sound of marching armies heard by the Philistines was caused by the wind blowing through branches and leaves of Poplar trees (also referred to as Mulberry tree in some text). The Poplar tree can grow to heights exceeding 150 feet. They have large, sturdy trunks that can measure up to eight feet in diameter. They grow and thrive in warm weather conditions. The leaves on the tree range in size and shape. Most of the leaves are oval to heart-shaped and have fine teeth along the edges. The leaves are green in the spring and summer and yellow and gold in thefall.

The bark of the tree is smooth and soft and range in color from white to dark gray. As the tree matures, the bark becomes rough and uneven. It can also crack and wrinkle depending on weather conditions. The life span of a Poplar tree is about 50 years.

One of the sounds that can be heard as the wind blew through the tree top can be referred to as whistling. Whistling is caused by the wind interacting on surfaces causing them to *resonate* at a given frequency dictated by their size. Most branches and twigs on a tree are not of equal length or thickness. These variations can cause lower or high pitch sounds. Another sound you might hear is referred to as rustling. It is caused by the leaves on the limbs and branches trying to tear off from strong winds. The other sound of rustling is the dried fallen leaves, or ground cover blowing around.

Leaf shapes and sizes affect sound

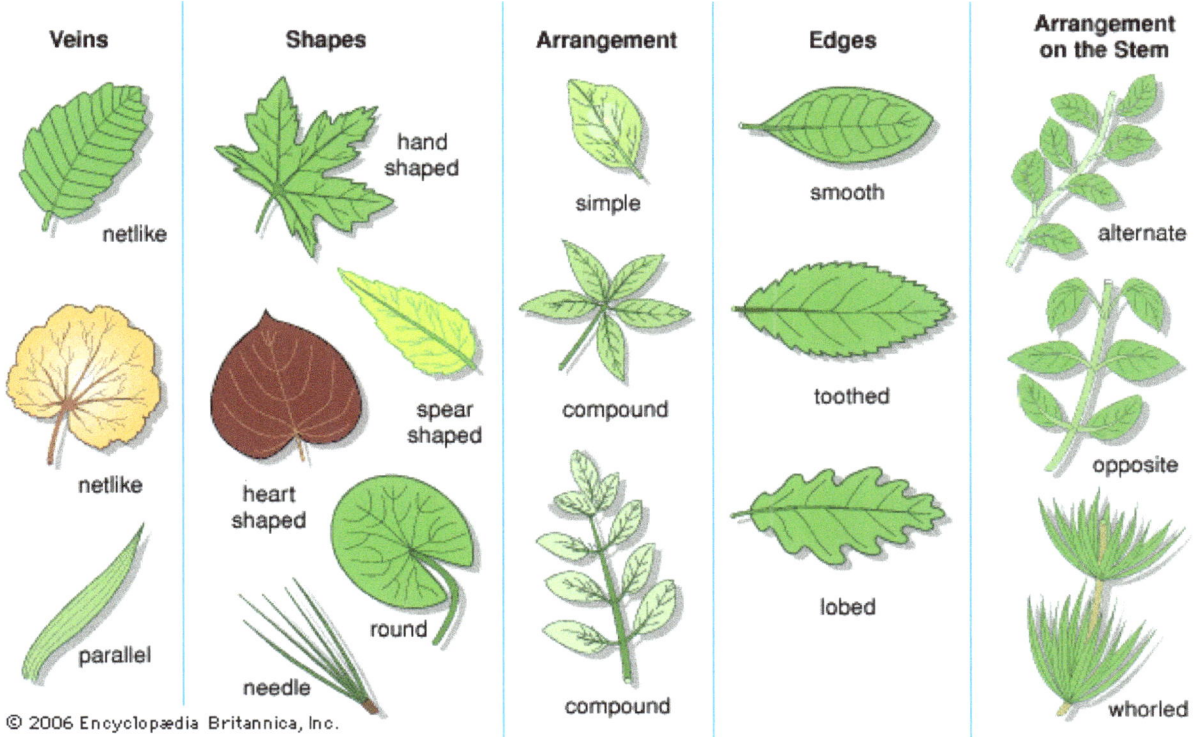

Leaf: natural shapes and arrangement. Art Britannica Online for Kids. Web. 22 Jan.2015

We hear howling of the wind through the trees because of the wind's velocity. The velocity causes the sound as it passes or move around or over objects. Also, the volume of air passing through a point is great during heavy winds creating louder sounds. The wind makes noise because air eddies [air moving in a circular movement, twist, swivel or whirlpool on the downwind side build and release periodically at audible frequencies.

Day Four: Great Lights in the Sky

And God said, "Let there be lights in the firmament of the heaven to divide the day from the night; and let them be for signs, and for seasons, and for days, and years And let them be for lights in the firmament of the heaven to give light upon the earth: and it was so. And God made two great lights; the greater light to rule the day, and the lesser light to rule the night: he made the stars also. And God set them in the firmament of the heaven to give light upon the Earth. And to rule over the day and over the night, and to divide the light from the darkness: and God saw that it was good. And the evening and the morning were the fourth day" (Genesis 1:14-19).

The light sources were essential as well as beneficial to humankind surviving and thriving. These celestial lights served humanity in the following ways: to regulate and manage the day; provide heat; initiate the start of the day; to give reflected light in the darkness of night; energy source for vegetation; establishing for signs for the Earth like the seasons and weather. A season is a period within defined by distinct weather. These light sources also play a vital role in influencing agriculture and human occupations; migration of birds and breeding of animals; circulation and movement of the wind, and for the calculation of definite times for months and years. (Genesis 8:22)

The fourth day introduces the ordinances and regulation of the luminaries called the Sun (the greater light), Moon (the lesser light), and the Stars regarding the Earth which is in the state of restoration. The purpose of the two great lights are to rule over the day and the night. They would regulate the length of light, the amount of light and darkness, and the intensity of their energy output (heat). The Stars rule the night equally with the Moon. However, Stars are greater producers of light and larger in size than the moon but the distance from the Earth is so far that they appear small and dim. The constellation of Stars also helps in mapping position and finding directions on Earth (Job 38:31-32; Deuteronomy 24:13; Joshua 1:4; Psalm 136:7-8).

Earth's Yellow Star : The Sun

The Sun is the center of our solar system. The Sun is essential to all forms of life on earth. It is the primary source of energy on Earth. It releases mainly thermal (heat) and radiant energy (Exodus 16:21; Mark 4:6; James 1:11). Energy can be defined as the ability or capacity to do work. Energy does not disappear. It can change into another form of energy. The different energy forms can be classified as either potential (stored up energy in molecules) or kinetic (energy of molecules in motion). A brief list of few forms of energies are chemical, mechanical, electrical, nuclear, and sound.

This giant ball of fire, the Sun, resembles a huge nuclear furnace fueled for it inner core. It is made up of extremely hot gases, mostly hydrogen and helium. Our Sun is also the brightest celestial body in the part of the universe we live in called the Milky Way. The Sun is a medium- sized yellow star. Hotter Stars are blue and cooler Stars are red (Psalm 89:34-37; Luke 23:25).

This yellow Star is the closet Star to Earth. It is about 93 million miles from the Earth.

It would take an Earth spaceship two-years to fly to the Sun. Some areas of the Sun are cool and appear as dark spots called sunspots. Flames can shoot up from the surface from 25, 000 miles to 50,000 miles into space called prominences. It takes about eight minutes and twenty seconds for light from the Sun to travel to the Earth's surface. The Sun rotates on its axis making a complete turn about every 25 days and circuit the entire heaven once each year. The Sun family consist of planets, Jupiter, Saturn, Uranus, Neptune, Venus, Earth, Mercury, Mars, that turn on their own axes and revolve around the Sun at different speeds (Psalm 19:1-6); Ecclesiastes; Judges 9:33.

Gravitation is the power that holds all these heavenly bodies in their own orbits in space with accuracy that you can read the sky (Psalm19:4)

A solar eclipse occurs when the Moon passes between the Sun and Earth, and the Moon fully or partially blocks the Sun. This happens only at a new moon when the Sun and the Moon are in an alignment with each other. In a total eclipse, the disk of the Sun is fully obscured by the Moon. In partial eclipses, only part of the Sun is obscured (Amos 8:9).

Crucifixion darkness

The Crucifixion darkness is recorded in three of the Gospels in which the sky becomes dark in daytime during the crucifixion of Jesus. Nature responded when members of humankind rejected Jesus and choose to put him to death.

Gospel of Mark account of the crucifixion, on the eve of Passover, it says that after Jesus was crucified at nine in the morning, darkness fell over all the land, or all the world from around noon "the sixth hour" until 3 o'clock "the ninth hour" (Mark :15: 33; Matthew 27:33; Luke 23:44). This darkness occurred at the brightest time of the day at noon.

Matthew recorded that during the darkness period it include an earthquake and the raising of the dead. "The Earth shook, and the
rocks were split. The tombs also were opened, and many bodies of the saints who had fallen asleep were raised."

The Passover Moon was at that time was in the full phase, so that it could not have been a normal eclipse. When it is full moon the moon cannot intervene between the earth and the sun. This observation can be explained as a supernatural rearrangement the Sun, Moon, and Earth and the atmosphere.

Another account of this event is given by Phlegon of Tralles, a Greek freedman of the Emperor Hadrian. Phlegon was a historical writer of the Olympiads. He stated," In the fourth year of the 202nd Olympiad, there was a great and remarkable eclipse of the sun, above any that had happened before. At the sixth hour, the day was turned into the darkness of night, so that Stars were seen in the heaven; and there was a great earthquake in Bithynia, which overthrew many houses in the city of Nicaea."

This ancient author, Dionysius the Areopagite (Acts. 17:34) says that he saw a solar eclipse phenomenon at Heliopolis, in Egypt, and he is reported to have exclaimed, "Either the God of nature, the Creator is suffering, or the universe dissolving ."Julius Africanus, who wrote about AD 221, In speaking of Jesus' crucifixion and the darkness that covered the land during this event, Africanus found a reference in the writings of Thallus that dealt with this cosmic report. Africanus asserts, "On the whole world there pressed a most fearful darkness, and the rocks were rent by an earthquake, and many places in Judea and other districts were thrown down. This darkness Thallus, the historian, in the third book of his History, states, "this appears to me without reason, an eclipse of the Sun."

*Julius Africanus, Extant Writings, XVIII in *The Ante–Nicene Fathers*, ed. by Alexander Roberts and James Donaldson (Grand Rapids: Eerdmans, 1973), vol. VI, p. 130, as cited in Gary R. Habermas, *The Historical Jesus: Ancient Evidence for the Life of Christ*, (Joplin, MO: College Press Publishing Company), 1996.]

"Lastly, the purported *Letter from Pontius Pilate to Tiberius* claimed the darkness had started at the sixth hour, covered the whole world and, during the subsequent evening, the full moon resembled blood for the entire night.

Life, as we know it on Earth, would be impossible without the Sun

- Light from the Sun provides a constant source of energy in the form of heat and light.
- Without the Sun's heat and light, the Earth would be a lifeless ball of ice coated rocks.
- Plants collect that energy and convert it into chemical energy in the process called photosynthesis. During this process, oxygen gas and water vapors are released to the atmosphere and glucose and other macronutrients are produced by the plant.

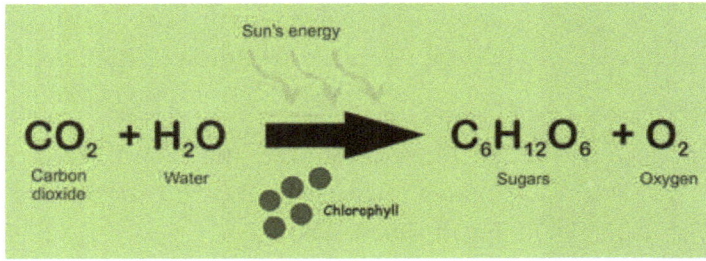

- The Sun influences our mood and emotional well-being (SAD-seasonal affective order)
- Sunlight also help our bodies to form Vitamin-D underneath the skin that maintains teeth, bones and helps the body to absorb calcium.
- The tilting of the Earth's axis and revolution each year (365 ¼ days) completes a revolution around the Sun, causing the seasons. The axis tilting toward the Sun brings summer in the Northern hemisphere. The axis tilts away, causing winter in the Southern hemisphere. The Equinox means equal length of night and day causing the vernal equinox (spring) and the autumnal equinox (autumn).
- Sunlight and darkness trigger the release of hormones (serotonin, melatonin) in

your brain.
- Sun exposure can help heal some skip disorders like eczema, acne, jaundice, and psoriasis.
- Researchers have discovered a compound called nitric oxide. This compound helps to lower blood pressure and is released into the blood vessels as soon as the skin is exposed to sunlight.

Establishment of seasons after the flood- Genesis 8:22	Season when King go to war 2 Samuel 11:1	Heating the Earth atmosphere creates the wind-
Birds know when to migrate – Jeremiah 8:7	Summer, Autumn, Winter – Zechariah 8:19	Creator determines the season – Daniel 2:20-21
Seedtime, harvest time – Genesis 8:22	Spring-new growth appears – Proverbs 27:25	Summer intense heat- Psalm 32:4
Summer- ripening fruit- Jeremiah 40:10-12 Summer, Winter -Psalm 74:17	The Earth spins in an eastward direction. This makes the Sun appear as if it is rising in the east and setting in the west.	The sun's heat causes water in the oceans, rivers, and lakes to evaporate and form water vapor - water cycle (Isaiah 55:10)

Seasons

Seasons occur because the Earth is titled on an imaginary axis 23.5 degree, the revolution Earth's movement around the Sun, and the direction of the North Pole.

The Earth is farthest from the Sun in July and is closest to the Sun at the beginning of January. It is the angle of the Sun's ray and the position in the sky that effects the temperature.

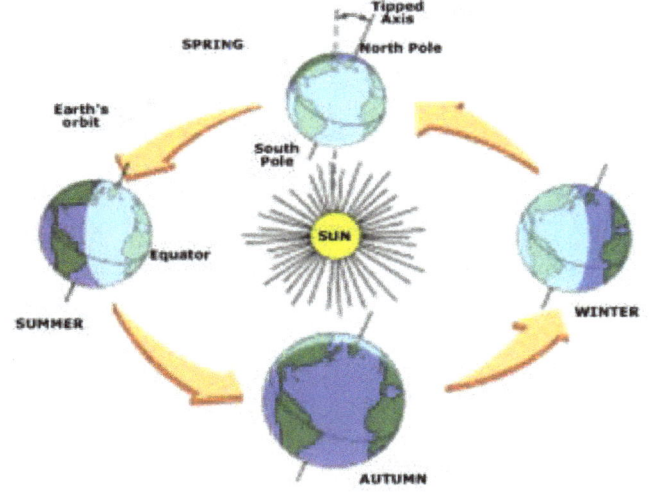

The North Pole always point in the same direction and never directly at the Sun because of the tilt. As the Earth revolves around the Sun one side of the Earth is always pointed or tilted towards the Sun. When the North Pole tiles toward the Sun it is summer time in the Northern Hemisphere and winter in the Southern Hemisphere.

When the North Pole tilts away from the Sun it is winter in the Northern Hemisphere and summer in the Southern Hemisphere. The Sun is highest in the sky during summer season and lower in the sky during winter season.

The Moon

The Earth's has only one natural satellite, the Moon. The brightest natural light you see at night is a natural reflector (Psalm 89:37). The Moon does not make any of its own light. It reflects about 7 percent of the sunlight that hits it. This reflected light is what we see. When the moon is full, it gives out its greatest amount of illumination.

The Moon appears to change shapes over time. It is not changing shapes but is traveling around the Earth. We see different part the Moon as light is reflected form the surface each night. The lighted part of the moon is facing the Sun. The part facing away from the Sun is dark.

The Moon's shapes are called phases. The phases of the Moon depend on the position of the Moon and the Sun. When the Moon and Sun are on the same side of the Earth, you cannot see it at all. When the Moon and Sun are on opposite side of the Earth, the Moon look like a bright circle. When the it looks like a half circle it is called a quarter moon. When the Moon looks like a smile on the side it is called a crescent moon. When the Moon looks like a deflated football it is called a gibbous moon.

The Moon travel or orbit around the Earth in 27days, 7 hours 43 minutes and 11.6 seconds. A lunar month is New Moon to New Moon about 29.5 days. It orbits counterclockwise in relationship to the Earth from west to east. The surface of the Moon has craters, lava plains, mountains and valleys. It has a very thin atmosphere and no ozone layer for protection from the Sun's harmful radiation. There is no weather. The footprints left behind by Apollo astronauts will remain visible on the Moon forever because there is not wind or erosion.

The Moon has a diverse temperature range from boiling hot to freezing cold. This is determined by its position with the Sun. The Moon tilt is less than that of the Earth's tilt. It is about 1.54 degrees. This means the moon does not have seasons like Earth does. However, because of the tilt, there are places at the lunar poles that never see daylight.

Phases of the Moon Relationship between Sun, Earth, and Moon

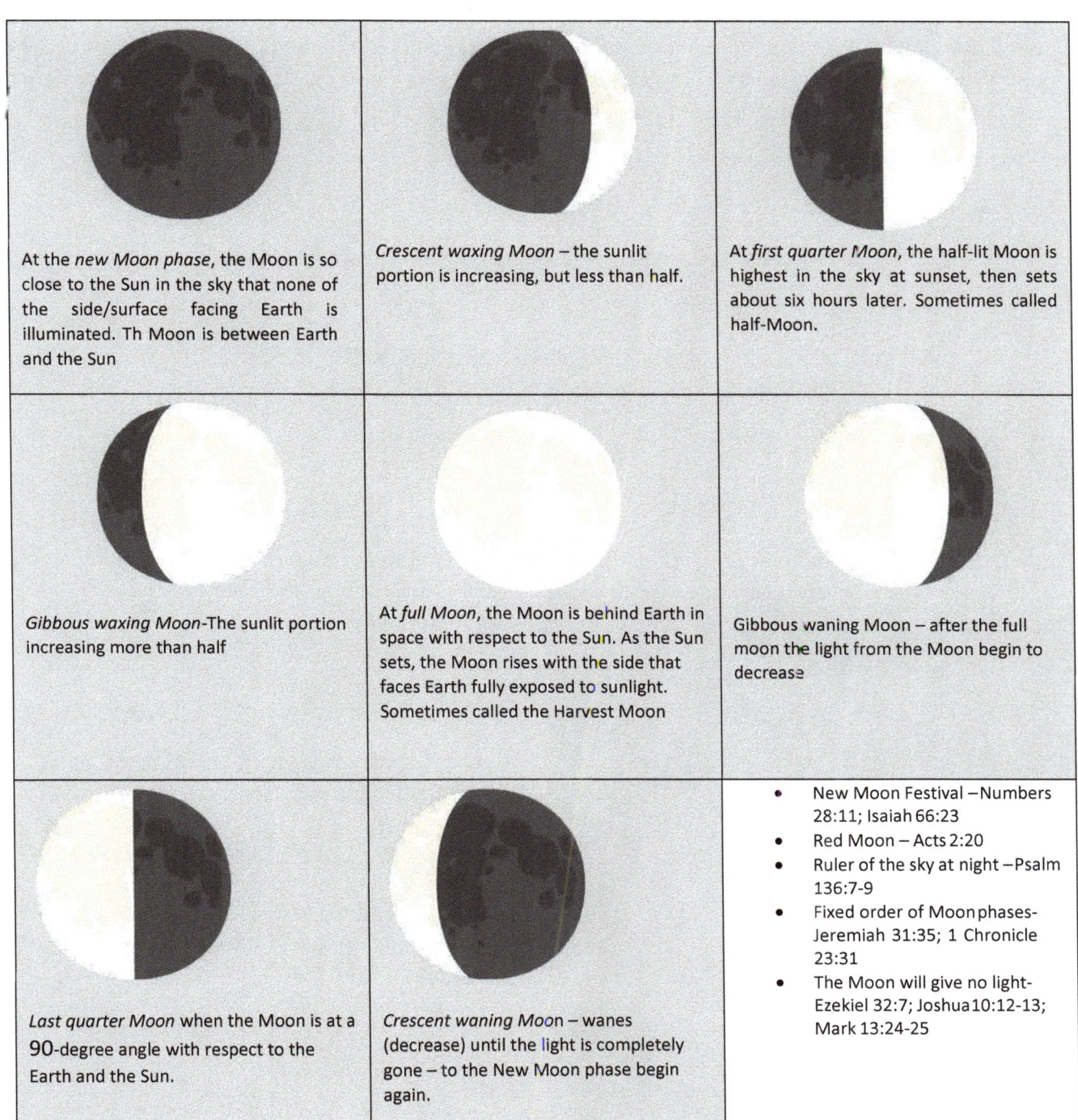

An eclipse of the Moon or lunar eclipse can only occur at full Moon, and only if the Moon passes through some portion of Earth's shadow. That shadow is composed of two cone-shaped components, one nested inside the other. The outer or penumbral shadow is a zone where the Earth blocks part but not all the Sun's rays from reaching the Moon. The inner or umbral shadow is a region where the Earth blocks all direct sunlight from reaching the Moon.

The Moon is beneficial to the Earth in the following ways"

- Act as a stabilizer for the Earth to spin on it axis
- Provides an accurate time keeping record based on the phases
- Tides are caused by gravitational attraction between Earth and the Moon
- Gregorian calendar is based on the Earth rotation and the Biblical calendar is determined by the Moon's position
- Provides light at night unless it is in a new moon phase

Twinkle, Twinkle, little Stars

All planets, including Earth, reflect light, just like the Moon. If they did not reflect light, we would not be able to see them. Like Earth, all planets orbit the Sun. They look like stars in the sky. You can often find the planet Venus just by looking for the brightest star-like object just before dawn or just after dark.

Most of the Stars you see in the night sky are huge fireballs far away. Stars make light by burning gases.

Astronomers looked for patterns in the stars. They used the stars to make dot to dot pictures of people and animals. We call these pictures constellations. Just as the Sun appears to rise in the east and set in the west each day, so do the Stars (Job 38:31- 32).

Day Five-Animals: Creeping, Crawling, Flying, Leaping, Swimming Things-

And God said, "Let the waters bring forth swarms of living creatures and let birds fly above the Earth across the dome of the sky." So, God created the great sea monsters and every living creature that moves, of every kind, with which the waters swarm, and every winged bird of every kind". And God saw that it was good. God blessed them, saying, "Be fruitful and multiply and fill the waters in the seas, and let birds multiply on the Earth". And there was evening and there was morning, the fifth day. And God said, "Let the Earth bring forth living creatures of every kind: cattle and creeping things and wild animals of the Earth of every kind: and it was so" (Genesis 1:20-25).

It appears many created operations occurred on the fifth day. Jehovah Elohim repopulated the sea, sky, and land. God created sea animals that included coral, squid, fish, and whales. He created the birds, bats, and other winged animals. Microbes, single celled organisms, like bacteria, fungi, algae, and protozoans were found in the water, on land, and in the guts of other organisms. Microbes are very important in recycling nutrients (carbon cycle, nitrogen cycle, water cycle) in our ecosystems and decomposing dead matter or tissues. The creeping things included some of the following members: insects and reptiles.

Restorative conditions provided sustainability

The Bible and scientific studies agree on the fundamental elements needed for the beginning of animal life. Both chemical and physical processes aided by the input of energy could have produced very simple cells (basic unit of life). Science says you need:

Organic Elements of Life

- (a) nonliving components (abiotic) small inorganic molecules like Carbon, Hydrogen, Nitrogen, Phosphorus, Oxygen;

- (b) the combination of small molecules or monomers called amino acids or nucleotides into large biomolecules of polymers (macromolecules) to make organic compounds like proteins, carbohydrates lipids, nucleotides;

- (c) the beginning of molecules surrounded by membrane like structures; and

- (d) and the formation of genetic materials like DNA and RNA needed for the ability to self-replicate. The first four days of restoration through the initiation of the Holy Spirit's energy-input in the dying Earth prepared all these conditions for life: the air, water, the land, and vegetation. Earth environment and atmosphere was ready for animals.

The dictionary and the science book define an animal as a multicellular organism. Some classification of animals includes protozoans (paramecium, amoeba, spirogyra) and other single-celled eukaryotes (cells that have a nucleus, complex organelles, and chromosomes). Protozoans have motility and animal-like nutritional modes. They take in oxygen and release carbon dioxide.

Animals are not plants (producers) but consumers because they do not make their own food nor do they have cell walls or contain chlorophyll for photosynthesis. Nor are they humans. Only humans were created in the image of God (Genesis 1:27). Animals were created out of the ground the LORD God formed every beast of the field and every fowl of the air (Genesis 2:19).

Animals have sense organs and nervous systems that help them to detect stimuli in the environment, free moving, actively acquiring food and digest food, have definite shapes, limited growth, and can move voluntarily. Animals can be herbivores (plant eaters only), carnivores (meat eaters mainly) and omnivores (eat plants and animals).

Divisions of Living things into Kingdoms

Scientists group living things into five large kingdoms of living things: monerans (bacterial cells), protists (diatoms, dinoflagellate), fungi (mushrooms, bread molds, lichen, mildew) plants (ferns, horsetails, fruit trees, grasses), and animals (crustaceans, mammals, arthropods, reptiles, and mollusks). The Animal Kingdom can be grouped into two main groups: the vertebrates and invertebrates. Animals without backbones are called invertebrates and consist of insects, spiders, crustaceans, mollusks, worms, and jellyfish. Vertebrates are animals with backbones and consists of fishes, amphibians, reptiles, birds, and mammals.

| *Monerans-simple and unicellular* | *Protists – unicellular* | *Fungi- unicellular or multicellular; absorb food* | *Plants- multicellular; make their own food; chloroplast cell wall* | *Animal- multicellular; obtain their own food* |
|---|---|---|---|---|//
| 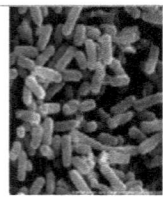 | 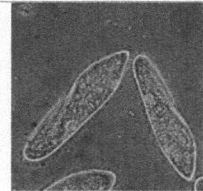 |  |  |  |

Adam and Eve, were assigned by God to be the cultivators or keepers of God's world and all the animals in it. Adam and Eve's first assignment was caring for the content and occupants in the Garden of Eden. Adam was also given the responsibility to name all the animals. He was the first taxonomist (Genesis 2:19-20). Taxonomy is the branch of science concerned with description identification, classification, and naming groups of biological organisms based on shared characteristics. The taxonomists organize living things in many ways using color, size, texture of skin covering, taste, habitat, and anatomy.

Taxonomists today give every living thing a two-part name that describes the kind of creature it is (species) and the group it belongs to (Genus) that has similar features and traits after their own kind. Humans would be called *Homo sapiens* which means 'wise man'. A good classification system should be meaningful to those using it and easily understood and easy to describe to someone else anywhere in the world.

Most likely Adam and Eve observed the animals before giving them a name that would reveal the essence of their nature. What might Adam and Eve observed from the animals that might help them in developing good relationships with each other and becoming good stewards toward all creation? Lessons from the boldness of the lions, modesty of a cat, grace in the fluttering of butterfly and the speed of humming bird's fluttering wings, the loyalty or devotion of dogs, swift action of a deer, and the industrious nature of ants at work.

Adam and Eve's position of glory and honor on Earth involved having dominion over animals can be summed up in the following verses, "What is mankind that you are mindful of them, humans being that you care for them? You made them rulers over the works of your hands; you put everything under their feet: all flocks and herds, and the animals of the wild, the birds in the sky and the fish in the sea, all that swim the path of the seas" (Psalm 8:4-8).

The Bible describes the character of animals, such as: wild (Job 39:15), ravenous (Isaiah 35:9), abominable (Ezekiel 8:10), noisome (Ezekiel 14:15), forbidden of worship (Deuteronomy 4:17), can be tamed (James 3:7), created not made (Genesis 1:24-25), as food (Genesis 9:2-3), classified as clean and unclean (Leviticus 11), and used as sacrifices (Genesis 4:4).

Microorganisms: It's a small world after all

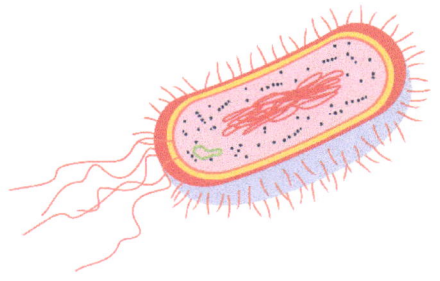

A new question to consider is where do microbes and viruses fit in the creation scenario? Life would be impossible without these invisible tiny organisms. Scientists like Leeuwenhoek, Pasteur, and Lister helped to bring the existence to our attention through the invention and use of the microscope. Microorganisms are not explicitly mentioned in the Scriptures but we can find evidence of the actions or processes produced because of their presence.

Microbes, plants, animals, and humans all live together. They are very small but essential to life and death. Microbes are single celled organism like bacteria, fungi algae, and protozoans. You will find them in water, on land, in the guts of other organisms, and even riding on the wind. We need them to help us digest food, acquire vitamins and minerals, breakdown complex nutrients such as nitrogen fixation in soil, and important in recycling materials throughout nature.

Examples might include:

- Leavening agent for bread making, yeast(fungi) -Genesis 14:18; Hosea 7:4
- Microorganism *Lactobacilli* for producing cheese – Job 10:10
- Dung – Intestinal microorganisms – Luke 13:8
- Fever -Matthew 8:14
- Mildew (plant disease) – Amos 4:9
- Plagues- Numbers 14:37
- Vinegar, wine and strong drinks (fermentation) – Ruth 2:14; Mark 5:23; Luke1:15
- Embalming – Genesis 50:2

Viruses are not microbes because they are not cells. Viruses have nonliving as well as living characteristics. They are thought of as disease-causing agents called pathogens. In biology, a pathogen (Greek: *pathos* 'suffering, passion' and 'producer of') that can produce diseases. Pathogens can produce toxins, enter tissues, colonize in animal and human body, hijack nutrients supply in the blood, and can suppress our immune system. Many theologians believe that pathogens surfaced after the fall of Adam and Eve and the curse of the ground (Genesis 3).

Gods loves Animals and He blessed them first

The Beatitudes was the sermon and teaching from Jesus on a mountain. He taught his disciples what it meant to be blessed. "And God blessed the animals, saying, be fruitful and multiply and fill the waters in the seas and let the fowls multiply in the Earth" (Genesis 1:22). This was the first blessings mentioned in scriptures. The blessing included fruitfulness, multiplication and occupancy of suitable habitats. God imparted reproductive powers or the powers of procreation for the Earth and the waters to be filled again (Psalm 128:3).

God is concerned for all His creation. He provides food for the cattle in the fields, for your raven why they call for food, and the lions that roar for their prey (Psalm 104:21). "Consider the ravens: they do not sow or reap they have no storeroom or barns, yet God feeds them. And how much more valuable you are than birds" (Luke 12:24).

The Bible instructs us to take care of animals under our charge. One of the signs of a righteous person is that they take care of their animals (Proverbs 12:10). The seventh day ordained by God as a day of rest also applies to the animals we own especially those that are beasts of burden.
They also need a refreshing and relaxing time.

God is concerned for all His creation. He provides food for the cattle and for the young raven when they call and the lion roars for their prey and seek their food from God (Psalm 104:21). "Consider the ravens: they do not sow or reap, they have no storeroom or barn, but God feeds them. And how much more valuable you are than birds!" (Luke 12:24). Or "Are not five sparrows sold for two pennies? Yet not one of them is forgotten by God" (Luke 12:6).

Animals as our first Teachers

Animals play a vital role in human harmony. They provide lessons of life for us as our teachers. In the book of Job, we find four sources of knowledge from the animals. "But ask the animals, and they will teach you, or the birds in the sky and they will tell you; or speak to the Earth, and it will teach you, or let the fish in the sea inform you. Which of all these does not know that the hand of the LORD has done this? In his hand is the life of every creature and the breath of all mankind" (Job 12:7-10).

"Go to the ant, you sluggard; consider its ways and be wise. It has no commander, no overseer or ruler, yet stores its provisions in summer and gathers it at food harvest. Ants are creatures of little strength, yet they store up their food in the summer; hyraxes (shrewmouse) are creatures of little power, yet they make their home in the crags; locusts have no king, yet they advance together in ranks; a lizard can be caught with the hand, yet it is found in kings' palace" (Proverbs 6:6-8; 30:25- 28).

The ant are remarkable insects that are intelligent and wise. They are social insects, highly industrialized, collect food in the proper (time) seasons; care for their young; work until the job is done; work for the good of the whole community; are carpenters of homes and underground tunnels; clean home; fight to death to defend their home and young from enemies; and carry out the work to be done without being forced by an overseer or ruler.

Animals used in Miraculous ways.

Animals are also used by God in miraculous ways. The story of the Prophet Balaam and the talking donkey: "Balaam got up in the morning saddled his donkey and went with the Moabite official. But God was very angry when he went, and the angel of the LORD stood in the road to oppose him. Balaam was riding on his donkey, and his two servants were with him. When the donkey saw the angel of the LORD standing in the road with a drawn sword in his hand, it turned off the road into a field. Balaam beat the donkey to get it back on the road. Then the angel of the LORD stood in a narrow path through the vineyards, with walls on both sides. When the donkey saw the angel of the LORD, it pressed close to the wall, crushing Balaam's foot against it. So, he beat the donkey again.

Then the angel of the LORD moved on ahead and stood in a narrow place where there was no room to turn, either to the right or to the left. When the donkey saw the angel of the LORD, it lay down under Balaam, and he was angry and beat it with his staff. Then the LORD opened the donkey's mouth (2 Peter 2:16), and it said to Balaam, "What have I done to you to make you beat me these three times" Balaam answered the donkey, "You have made a fool of me! If only I had a sword in my hand, I would kill you right now." The donkey said to Balaam, "Am I not your own donkey, which you have always ridden, to this day? Have I been in the habit of doing this to you?" "No," he said. Then the LORD opened Balaam's eyes, and he saw the angel of the LORD standing in the road with his sword drawn. So, he bowed low and fell facedown. The angel of the LORD asked him, "Why have you beaten your donkey these three times? I have come here to oppose you because your path is a reckless one before me. The donkey saw me and turned away from me these three times. If it had not turned away, I would certainly have killed you by now, but I would have spared it." (Numbers 22:21-32)

Animals as Pets

Many homes across the world have the presence of animals: cats, dogs, pigs, turtles, goldfish, parakeets, chickens, and hamsters. The Bible does not give much information on keeping pets. Dogs are sometimes referred to as 'man's best friend. The Hebrew name for dog is *kelev,* which derived from *kulo lev* which means 'all heart'.

One example of a loving pet owner is from the Prophet Nathan telling King David a parable: There were two men in a certain town, one rich and the other poor. The rich man had a very large number of sheep and cattle; but the poor man had nothing except one little ewe lamb he had bought. He raised it, and it grew up with him and his children. It shared his food, drank from his cup and even slept in his arms. It was like a daughter to him (2 Samuel 12:1-3).

Survey of THE ANIMAL KINGDOM

The animal kingdom consists of animals from the simple to the complex. The more complex the organism will consist of tissues and organs that form into organ systems (circulatory, digestive, nervous).

Invertebrates

Sponges	Coelenterates	Flatworms	Roundworms
- pore covered body with a skeletal structure for support -no head end, no mouth, no tissues or organs - digestion by collar cells	- cylinder shaped body like an umbrella - radial symmetry - tentacles with stinging cells for protecting -includes coral, jellyfish, sea anemones, sea fans	- bilateral symmetry -three cell layers -Digestive cavity -one opening -include tapeworm, planarians	-tubular body with bilateral symmetry -a digestive tract with two opening -sexual reproduction Includes- hookworms, pinworms, trichinae
Wheel Animals				**Segmented Worms**
- these animals live in lakes, rivers, and ocean -cylindrical or vase-shaped -crown of cilia -complete digestive system				- three cell layers -tube-within a tube body plan - pair of bristles or setae on each body segment -includes earthworms, leeches

Mollusks

These animals mainly obtained their food and oxygen from the water that flows through their bodies. Mollusks have soft, moist bodies with no bones. They have hard shells for protection. Most mollusks live in water. Those that live on land make slime to move on. Mollusks are good sources of food and use to make jewelry.

Bivalves	Gastropods	Cephalopods
-These animals have a shell consisting of two hinged valves and a muscular foot -includes clams, oysters, and mussels, scallop	-These animals are "belly footed with a one-coiled shell - includes snails, slugs	These animals have a well-developed head and a foot -divided into many arm-like tentacles - includes octopuses and squids
	Psalm 58:8 -used for blue and purple dyes - Esther 8:15; Numbers 15:38; Exodus 28:4-5 -Lydia was a seller of purple	

Arthropods

Arthropods have jointed appendages, segmented bodies, and exoskeleton. There are five major classes.

Echinoderms

Arachnids	Crustaceans	Chilopod	Diplopods	Insects	(Echinoderms)
-arachnids have eight legs. -includes spiders, scorpion	-Crustacean have chewing jaws and a pair of appendages on each segment of the thorax - crabs, lobsters, shrimps	-centipedes have flat bodies and one pair of legs per body segments	-millipedes have rounded bodies and two pairs of legs per body segment	-insects have three distinct body parts: head, thorax, and abdomen; three pairs of legs. -includes bees, beetles, butterflies, flies, grasshoppers	-a water vascular system -an internal skeleton -radial symmetry -spiny skin -tube feet -includes starfish, sand dollars, brittle stars, sea urchins, sea cucumbers
Spider-Isaiah 59:5-6 **Scorpion** – Deuteronomy 8:15			**Millipede**-Leviticus 11:41-42	**Bee**- Judge 14:7-8 **Fly**- Ecclesiastic 10:1 **Gnat (mosquito)**- Exodus 8:17 **Ant**- Proverbs 30:24 **Cicada**- Deut. 28:43	

Vertebrates

Jawless Fishes	Cartilaginous Fishes	Bony Fishes
Hagfish, Lamprey	Rays, Sharks	Trout, Tilapias, Flounders
-Rasping mouth to fore holes -Cartilaginous skeleton	-cold bloodedness -jawed, respiration through gills	- Ate fish in Egypt-Numbers 11:5 - fins and scales – Leviticus 11:9-12 - small fish – Matthew 15:34-38 -great fish – Jonah 1:17 -many kinds of fish -Ezekiel 47:10

Amphibians	Reptiles
Frogs, Salamanders, Toads	
-lives part of their lives in water and part on land - lays eggs without shells in moisture -Life cycle involves metamorphosis -absorption of oxygen through the skin - uses gills in water and lungs on land -Exodus 8:2-3 -Psalm 105:30 - Psalm 78:45	- have scales that contain protein to protect the skin from desiccation and abrasion - -most lay their shelled eggs on land - -cold-blooded - Have amniotic eggs and rib-cage - Chameleon, lizard, tortoise – Leviticus 11:29-30 - Serpent – Job 26:13 - Dragon – Deuteronomy 32:3 - Asp – Psalm 58:4

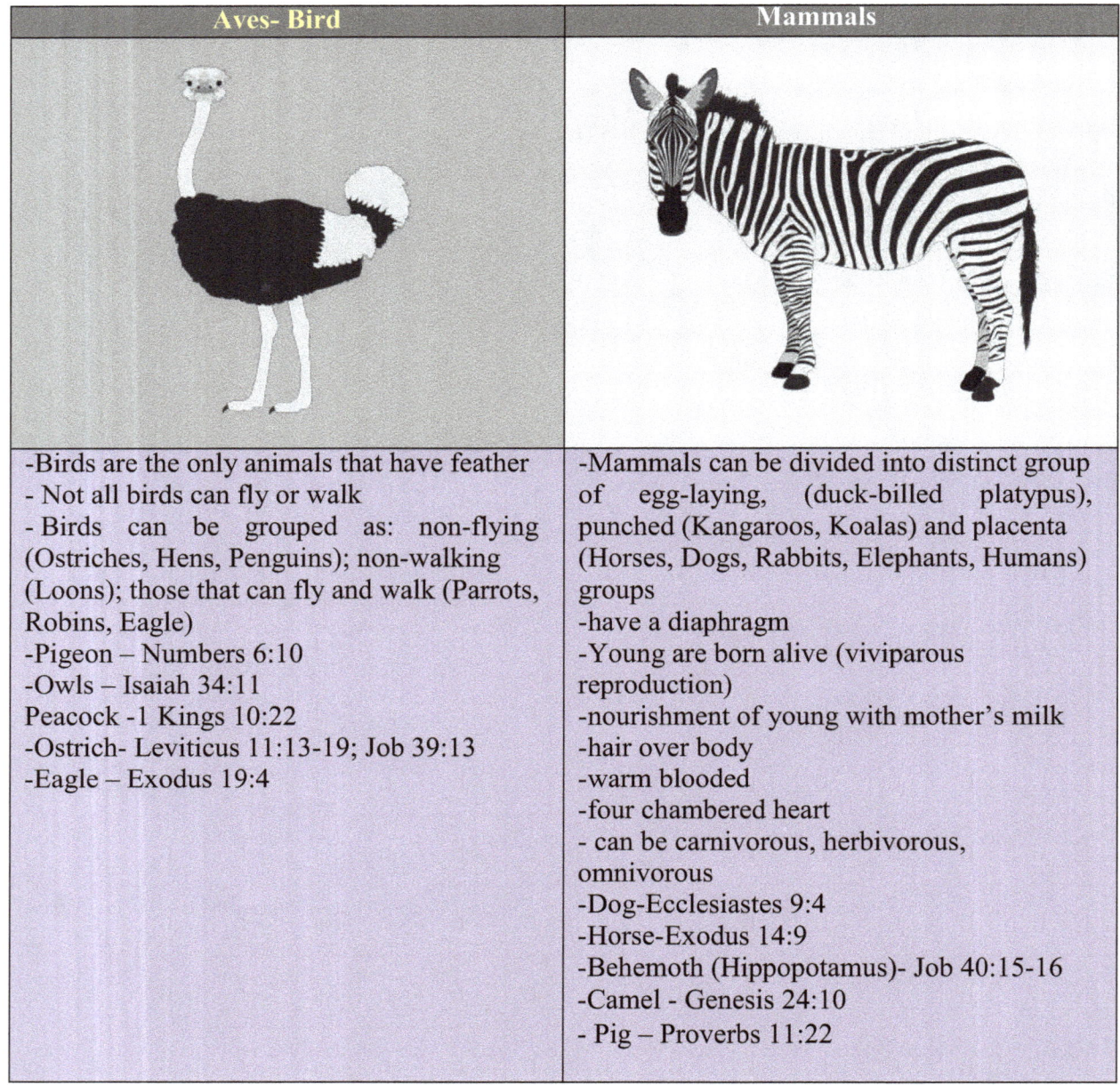

Aves- Bird	Mammals
-Birds are the only animals that have feather - Not all birds can fly or walk - Birds can be grouped as: non-flying (Ostriches, Hens, Penguins); non-walking (Loons); those that can fly and walk (Parrots, Robins, Eagle) -Pigeon – Numbers 6:10 -Owls – Isaiah 34:11 Peacock -1 Kings 10:22 -Ostrich- Leviticus 11:13-19; Job 39:13 -Eagle – Exodus 19:4	-Mammals can be divided into distinct group of egg-laying, (duck-billed platypus), punched (Kangaroos, Koalas) and placenta (Horses, Dogs, Rabbits, Elephants, Humans) groups -have a diaphragm -Young are born alive (viviparous reproduction) -nourishment of young with mother's milk -hair over body -warm blooded -four chambered heart - can be carnivorous, herbivorous, omnivorous -Dog-Ecclesiastes 9:4 -Horse-Exodus 14:9 -Behemoth (Hippopotamus)- Job 40:15-16 -Camel - Genesis 24:10 - Pig – Proverbs 11:22

"So, God created mankind in his own image, in the image of God he created them; male and female he created them. God blessed them and said to them, "Be fruitful and increase in number; fill the Earth and subdue it. Rule over the fish in the sea and the birds in the sky and over every living creature that moves on the ground" (Genesis 1:24-28).

Plants and animals were created before humans. There is great diversity among these living things starting with the microscopic phytoplankton (microscopic algae and cyanobacteria) and zooplankton (small, drifting animals). One of the greatest lessons we learn from the early created organisms are their similarities and differences when compared to God creatures designed to give him glory, the humans. Just as Adam did (Genesis 1: 19-20), scientists today classified all living things into groups called phylum. Phyla are large groups of organisms with the same body plan.

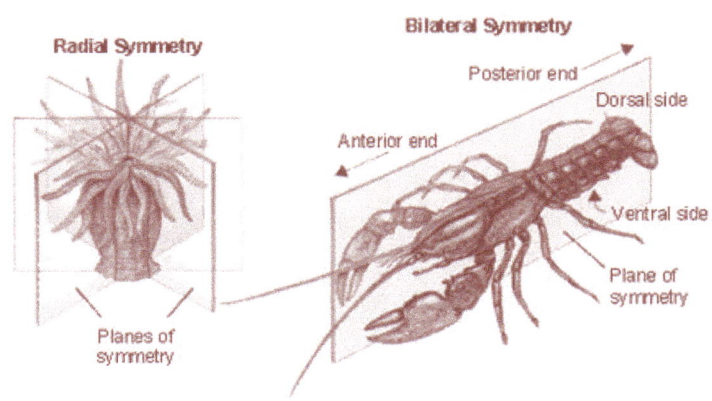

Symmetry is the balanced distribution of duplicate body parts, forms, size, shapes within the body of an organism.

Asymmetric symmetry lack of equal arrangement like a sponge. Radial symmetry is a basic body plan in which the organism can be divided into similar halves by passing an imaginary plane at any angle along a central axis. Examples of such Organisms are those that are sessile (anchored in one place) and ocean bottom-dwelling animals (starfish, sea anemone, jelly fish). Bilateral symmetry a basic plan in which left and right sides of the organism can be divided into mirror images along a midline (bear, human).

A possible explanation of animals' diversity plan during the created process follows this arrangement:

- One cell organism
- No true tissues organism- Asymmetry
- Radial symmetry
- True tissues organism
- Bilateral symmetry
- Brain formation
- Distinct Head end
- Vertebral column
- Jaws
- Lungs or lung derivates
- Lobed fins
- Four legs
- Amniotic egg
- Milk producing gland for young

There is a unique unity of all living things. Animals and humans ingest food for nutrition, have body cavities and membrane, they respire, have a mode of movement, reproductive cells, method of removal of wastes, cells to receive stimuli, a means of assimilation materials for metabolic healthiness, and they were both made from the ground (Genesis 1:24; 2:7). However, will all these similarities, human beings, are the most outstanding creation of God before He rested from all his work on the seventh day (Genesis 2:3).

Animals have greater physical abilities that supersede human capacities. Cheetahs are the fastest land animals that can travel 68-75mph and Peregrine Falcon are the fastest bird or animal that can travel at a speed of 242 mph. Eagles, Hawks, and Buzzards can scan the Earth from a height of 10-15,000 feet and spot a prey, dive in at 100 mph and never lose sight of the targeted meal. Owls can swirl their heads around 270 degrees increase their field of vision. Silvertip Grizzles can smell you and your fear up to 18 miles away and over time. Dolphins can hear 18 times better than humans and wax moths have extreme hearing of up to frequencies of 300 kHz while humans can hear about 20 kHz.

Animals only live to feed to survive and reproduce. Animals are more powerful than human in many ways, nevertheless, Adam and Eve were given dominion over them (Genesis 1: 28-29). However, human purpose in life goes beyond survival, beyond speed, beyond hearing, beyond seeing to the utmost of praise that will lead to a personal relationship with God. Humans were created in the image of God with the ability of abstract thinking, language, express emotions, moral judgement, responsible for the origin of sin in the world, consciousness, personality with the development of a higher brain activity, has a body, soul, and God puffed his spirit into their bodies. The only other created beings with a spirit are Angels.

Sixth Day- Large Animals and Humanity Created

And God said, "Let the land produce living creatures according to their kinds: the livestock, the creatures that move along the ground, and the wild animals, each according to its kind." And it was so God made the wild animals according to their kinds, the livestock according to their kinds, and all the creatures that move along the ground according to their kinds. And God saw that it was good. Then God said, "Let us make mankind in our image, in our likeness, so that they may rule over the fish in the sea and the birds in the sky, over the livestock and all the wild animals, and over all the creatures that move along the ground." So, God created mankind in his own image, in the image of God he created them; male and female he created them. God blessed them and said to them, "Be fruitful and increase in number; fill the Earth and subdue it. Rule over the fish in the sea and the birds in the sky and over every living creature that moves on the ground" (Genesis 1:24-28).

"And the LORD **formed** (Heb. *yatsar*- to mold or squeeze into shape as a potter) man of the **dust** (Heb. *aphar*- mud, rubbish, powder, clay, ashes) of the ground and **breathed** (Heb. *naphach*-to breathe out, puff, inflate) into his nostrils the **breath** (Heb. *neshamah*- the air inhaled and exhaled, respiration) of **life** (the body, soul, and spirit live and function together) and man (Adam) **became** (Heb. *hayah*-came to pass) **a living soul** (Heb.-*nephesh*-that which breathes, the inner being of man) " (Genesis 2:7).

So, the man gave names to all the livestock, the birds in the sky and all the wild animals. But for Adam no suitable helper was found. Then, the Lord God caused the man to fall into a deep sleep; and while he was sleeping, he took one of the man's ribs and then closed (*first anesthesia and major operation*) the incision with flesh. Then the Lord God **made** (Heb. *panah*- builder, designer, skillfully formed) a woman from the rib he had taken out of the man, and he brought her to the man. The man said, "This is now bone of my bones and flesh of my flesh; she shall be called **'woman,'** (Heb. *ish shah*-she-man, womb-man,) for she was taken out of man (Heb. *ish*)."

The five basic needs of both men and woman from the environment are oxygen, water, food shelter, and warmth. Everything around them encompasses their environment and would positively or negatively affect their lives.

The third creative act of God brought the larger animals and humanity were brought into existence. Their bodies were formed but their lives were created. This new creature was called Adam. In the Hebrew language, Adam means ruddy: to flush or turn rosy or red. This denotes Adam's origin, as being from the dust of the ground or red soil. Biologists and geologists have examined the composition of dust/soil and have discovered the relationship between chemical makeup of human and the chemical composition of the ground, celestial bodies, the atmosphere, and the ocean. All these agents made contributions to the formation of dust during both ancient and modern times.

Volcanic Eruption- source of 'dust'

Dust comes from various sources such as volcanic eruptions, atmospheric dust, from dry and barren regions with high velocity winds, ashes from plant pollen, animal hairs, erosion, mineral fragments, and remains of burnt-out meteors, shedding of dead cells from the skin, grazing animals, cosmic dust, and other materials found in the local environment.

Volcanic eruptions are responsible for releasing molten rock or lava from deep within the Earth. The gases and dust particles thrown into the atmosphere. Most of the particles spewed from the volcanoes cool the planet by temporarily shading incoming solar radiation.

Even though volcanoes are in specific places on Earth (basins in the Pacific Ocean) their effects can be more widely distributed in the form of gases, dust particles, and ashes into the atmosphere. Because of atmospheric circulation patterns eruptions in the tropics can influence northern and southern atmospheres.

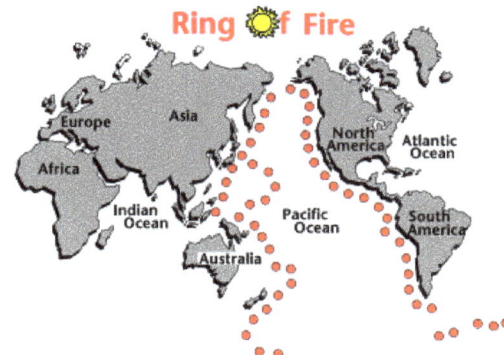

The bodies of living things like plants and animals are made from the same basic building materials that form the rocks, water, and gas. Some other non-living things needed for life are elements like carbon, hydrogen, oxygen, nitrogen and other trace elements in small but essential amounts. Let us examine one dust/soil producing agent. Deep within the Earth, molten rock, called magma mixes with gases. The magma begins to rise toward Earth's surface and erupts through a weak area in the crust. These eruptions can occur as violent explosion, propelling lava hundreds of feet into the air.

The dirt/soil near volcanoes is very rich in minerals. The areas around volcanoes are some of the most fertile lands on Earth. These areas provide enrichment and nutrition for a variety of life forms. A short sample of life form such as microbes, decomposers, microorganisms, fungi, plants can as exist in mutual partnership with nature. They obtain heat energy from the sun, nutrients from the rocks that have decomposed and recombined into soluble molecules, by

chemical reaction to moisture and gases such as carbon dioxide from the atmosphere. Dirt/soil is formed from the interaction of climate, organism, relief, and time.

Atmospheric circulation and distribution of Soil

Soil is called the skin of the Earth. It interfaces with the lithosphere, the hydrosphere, atmosphere, and the biosphere. Soil exist in three states system: soil (minerals organic matter), liquid (water- soil solution), gases (porous hold gases; the soil atmosphere).

Atmospheric circulation is a large movement of air around the globe. The combination of atmospheric circulation with ocean circulation (direct movement of seawater generated by outside forces) together they move thermal energy (provided by radiant energy of the Sun) on the surface of the Earth. This motion called wind may be vertical, as when warm air rises. It can also be horizontal. Wind is created by air moving from high pressure areas, where air is densely compressed, to low-pressure areas, where air is less dense. Horizontal winds follow curved paths to due to the rotation of the Earth. "The wind blows where it wishes. You hear its sound, but you do not know where it comes from or where it is going. So, it is with everyone born of the Spirit" (John3:8); "As you do not know the path of the wind, or how the body is formed in a mother's womb, so you cannot understand the work of God, the Maker of all things" (Ecclesiastes 11:5).

Atmospheric forces cause the air to move. On a weather map, pressure differences are demarcated by parallel lines called isobars that show changes in pressure.

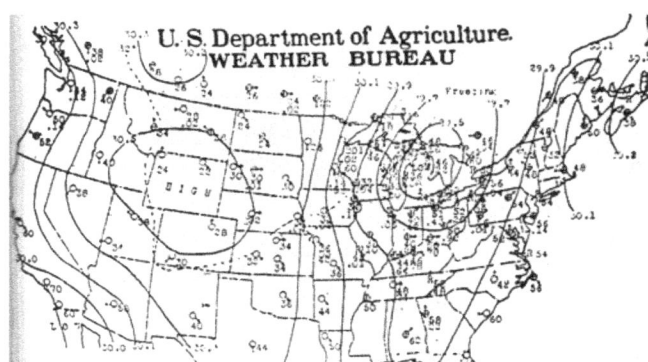

Materials that make their way from volcanic eruptions into the atmosphere are particles of dust and ash, sulfur dioxide, and greenhouse gases like water vapors and carbon dioxide. Small particles of dust get into the stratosphere and can travel vast distances, even worldwide. Volcanic ash is a mixture of shattered rocks lava), minerals, and quenched glass (magma).

The soil near volcanoes is among the richest and most fertile on Earth. Life forms exist in partnership with heat from the Sun, nutrients from rocks that have been decomposed and recombined into soluble molecules by chemical reactions to moisture and gases such as carbon dioxide from the atmosphere call chemical weathering.

Dirt/soil consistency can be hard, loose, firm, plastic, or sticky. Dirt covers or serves as a boundary to the lithosphere (the rigid outer part of the Earth consisting of the crust and upper mantle); close contact and connection to the hydrosphere (water found on, under, over the surface of the Earth); interacts with the atmosphere (the air surrounding the Earth); and the biosphere.

The Color of Soil

Dirt/Soil consist of four constituents: minerals material, organic material air, and water. The three mineral parts of soil are sand, slit, and clay. The largest component of soil is the mineral portion by 45-49% of the volume.

Soil color can be described as red, brown, yellow, yellowish-red, grayish-brown, pale red, and white. Organic matter (humus) manganese (form black mineral deposits) and iron (forms small crystals with a yellow or red color and decomposes into black humus) are the primary coloring agents in soil. Dark brown color in soil indicates that the soil has a high organic matter content. Wet soil appears darker than dry soil. However, the presence of water also affects soil color by affecting the oxidation rate. Soil that has a high-water content will have less air in the soil.

The red color of soil is due to iron oxides. Red soil is found in Africa, Asia, South American, and southwest North America. Soils form from the interaction of climate, organisms, parent materials, relief, and time. Red soil is a type of soil that
develops in a warm, temperate moist climate under deciduous or mixed forest. This soil type has thin inorganic and organic- mineral layers overlying a yellowish-brown leached layer. Yellow soil indicates the presence of oxidized ferric iron oxides. Dark brown or black color in soil indicates that the soil has a high organic matter content.

Soil conservation – the Skin of the Earth

Our skin covers almost every area of the human body. Skin serves the body by noting changes in our environment through sensation; protection barrier from bacteria invasion; temperature regulation controlling cooling and heating; excretion of unproductive gases and licuid waste, and interacting with the Sun to produce Vitamin D.

The dirt/soil is called the skin of the Earth and resembles in function the skin of the human body. It anchors all life on Earth. It is full of multiple organisms that live together as an ecosystem (a biological network of interacting organisms and their physical environment) and provide resources for all creation. The dirt/soil covering protects the Earth by absorbing the Sun's energy and reflecting the heat back into the atmosphere; holding or anchoring vegetations with the top layer; serves as a reservoir for water; provide a bank of food and fibers for smaller organisms.

Unfortunately, humanity abuse the land by over farming; erosion that will increase pollution or our water streams; reducing the production of fish and using land as chemical waste dumping grounds.

Establishing the Foundation for Life

The first six periods of the creative process established the foundation for life to thrive successfully on Earth. Days one and two formed the inorganic materials through a natural process that were not connected to any form of life. Most of the Earth is inorganic which includes rocks, minerals, metals, stone, glass, clay, water, and carbon dioxide. Generally, inorganic materials do not contain the element carbon. An element is a pure substance that cannot be broken down into other types of substances. The chemical and physical properties of one element differ from any other element.

Before the renewal of things like light, Sun, Moon, Earth, plants, living creatures there was water (Genesis 1:2b). Perhaps God used water with the dust to make clay and form Adam (Genesis 2:7).

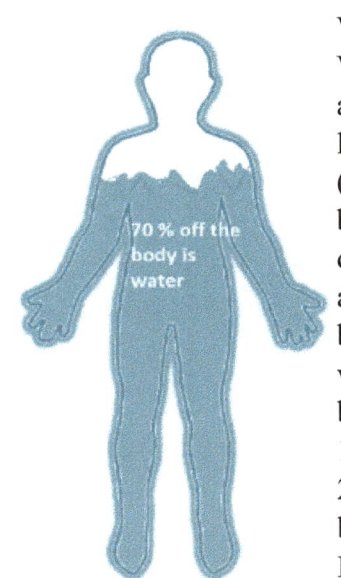

Water is an excellent example of an essential inorganic compound. Water is important because it makes up as much as 70 percent of an adult body and covers about 75 % of the Earth. Water serves as a lubricant (Proverbs 25:25; Exodus 7:24), cushion, insulator, cleanser (Ezekiel 36:25; John 13:10); and transporter of vital nutrients in the body. Water is called the universal solvent because it mixes easily and dissolves most things. Other groups of the inorganic compound that are essential to the body include salts, minerals, vitamins, acids, and bases. Salts are valuable ("Can that which is unsavory be eaten without salt? Or is there any taste in the white of an egg?"-Job 6:6) because that form minerals that builds strong teeth and bones (Ezekiel 16:4). Acids and bases in the body help to kill microbes (2 Kings 2:22); and breaks down food for digestion and assimilation for the body cells.

Days three through six (Genesis 1:19-31) formed the organic materialization of living organisms. Organic matter contains mainly carbon and hydrogen. The most abundant element in the universe is hydrogen. Carbon is the most abundant element by mass in the human body. Carbon can readily form very strong and uniform bonds with most elements. These compounds can make up cells and other structures that help in your life processes. Hydrogen and carbon bind together to form carbohydrates (sugars and starches) and lipids (triglycerides/fats). When you add nitrogen and sulfur to this combination you get amino acids. When amino acids connect and form long chains it is the initiation of making proteins. Add some phosphorus and nucleotides are form. The nucleotides bond together to produce nucleic acids called DNA and RNA.

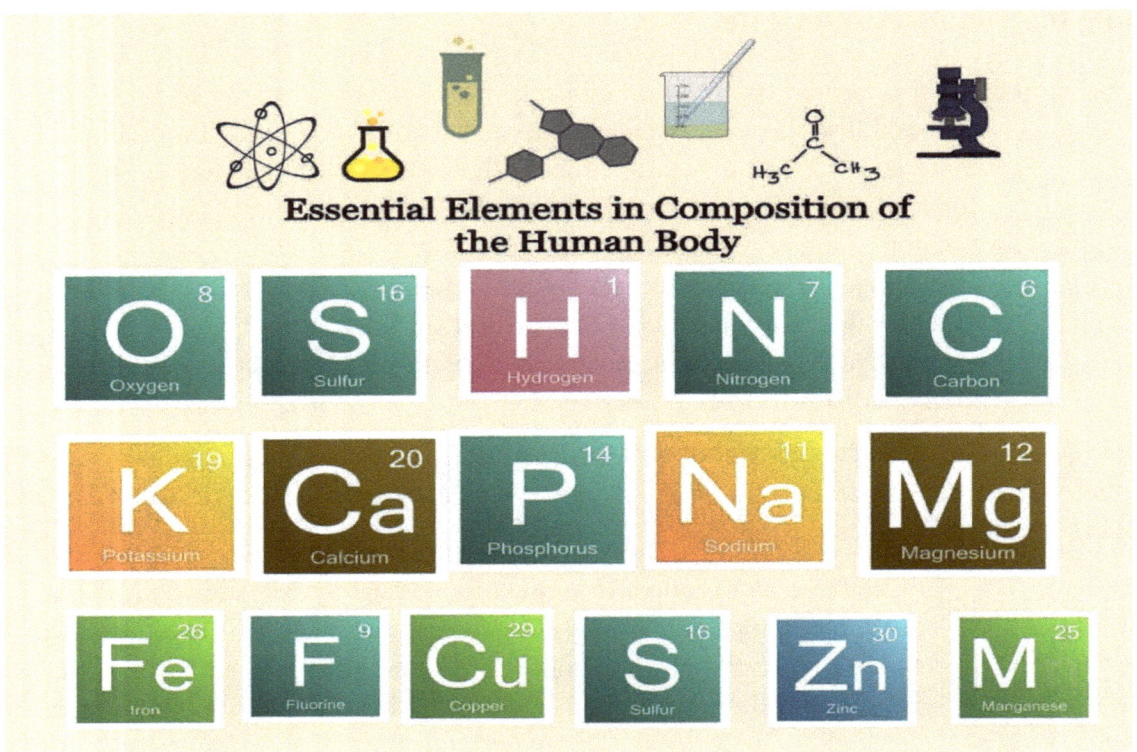

In the beginning God used small sizes and quantity and limited the number of components to create complex structures that rested on the foundation of a few essential element.

- **Oxygen-** 65% of your body's weight; aerobic respiration used in mitochondria to make ATP (energy); found in organic molecules; large amount in lungs and bloodstream; binds to hemoglobin in red blood cells; combines with Hydrogen to make water
- **Sulfur** – found in amino acids to build proteins
- **Hydrogen-** 10% of body weight; involved in critical chemical reactions of forming and breaking chemical bonds; binds with Oxygen to form water; found in all organic molecules
- **Nitrogen-** 3% of body weight; obtain from eating plants or herbivores; needed in protein synthesis for nucleic acids (DNA, RNA)
- **Carbon** – 18% of body weight; makes up molecules base for organic compounds
- **Potassium** – forms electrolytes in blood for maintaining muscular and nervous systems; regulates the heartbeat
- **Calcium-** 1.4 % of body weight; mostly found in the bones and teeth; needed in muscular contraction and protein regulation
- **Phosphorus-** 1% of body weight; found in bones, teeth, nucleic acids and energy molecules

- **Sodium**- essential in nerve transmission and muscle function
- **Magnesium** – enzyme cofactor; binds to ATP and nucleotides; used to build healthy teeth and bones
- **Iron**--enzyme cofactor; synthesis of hemoglobin and electron carriers; component of blood and used in Oxygen transport
- **Fluorine** - maintenance of tooth structure
- **Copper-**important as an electron donor in biological reaction; regulates Iron transport
- **Zinc-**essentials trace element that helps to regulate genes
- Manganese-essential for certain enzymes that protect the mitochondria

Organic materials formed in nature are built up over time by nutrients cycles. A few examples of organic matters are wood paper, textile, animal parts, DNA, and plants. Living organisms all contain carbon and other compounds. As they die and decompose they are broken down into simple structures and can be recycle back to the Earth.

These two components, inorganic and organic materials, are interdependent on each other. Elements found in the human body can be found in the Earth's crust.

Time -Line Connecting Inorganic and Organic creation components

Scientist use rock formations or fossils to identify boundaries in the Earth and to mark the first appearance of different forms of life in different strata (Genesis 1).

**millions and millions of years ago- the dateless past

**Hadean Eon 4500 mya	<ul><li>Formation of solar system</li><li>Moon forms</li><li>Earth formation complete</li><li>Liquid water on Earth</li></ul>	
Archean Eon 3800 mya	<ul><li>First oceans</li><li>heavy bombardment of asteroids and other celestial bodies from space</li><li>Abiotic synthesis of small organic molecules (amino acid, nucleotides, proteins)</li><li>Origin of life</li><li>Photosynthetic cells</li><li>Oxygen revolution- increase in the atmosphere</li></ul>	
Proterozoic 2500 mya	<ul><li>First cyanobacteria</li><li>First rock containing oxygen from the atmosphere and ocean</li><li>First eukaryotic fossils</li><li>First red algae</li><li>First lichen-like organisms</li><li>Ocean completely oxygenated</li><li>First bilaterally symmetric animals</li><li>First sponges</li><li>Soft-bodies invertebrates</li></ul>	

Cambrian 542 mya	• First comb jellies, arthropods, echinoderm	
Ordovician 488 mya	• Colonization of the land • First land plants • First fungi • First cartilaginous fish	
Silurian 443 mya	• First bony fish • Diversity of vascular plants	
Devonian 416 mya	• First insects • First fish with jaws • First tree-sized plants • First winged-insects • First amphibians • First seed plants- plants with leaves	
Carboniferous 360 mya	• First reptiles • First seed plants • Extensive forest of vascular plants	
Permian 299 mya	• First vessels in plants	
Triassic 251 mya	• First dinosaurs • Cone-bearing plants -Gymnosperms	
Jurassic 199 mya	• First mammals • First bird • Gymnosperms dominant	
Cretaceous 145 mya	• First Angiosperm-flowering plants • First placenta mammals • Dinosaurs become extinction at end of this period	
Paleogene 65 mya	• First horse, primate, rabbits • First whales • First apes	
Neogene 23 mya to present	• Earliest hominis • Ice age • Homo sapiens- human appear	

The Adam Experience
The Puff-Respiration (Genesis 2:7)

Respiration is the action of breathing. Breathing is the process that moves air in (inhalation) and out (exhalation) the lungs. This is called ventilation. Respiration begins with the nose. Our nose helps to filter and trap dust particles and microorganisms with mucus and hair. Air that you breathe in is warmed by capillaries inside the nasal cavities. This helps to prepare the air before it enters the lungs. The function of the respiratory system is to take oxygen out of the incoming air we breathe and to remove carbon dioxide from the blood and then release it out the body.

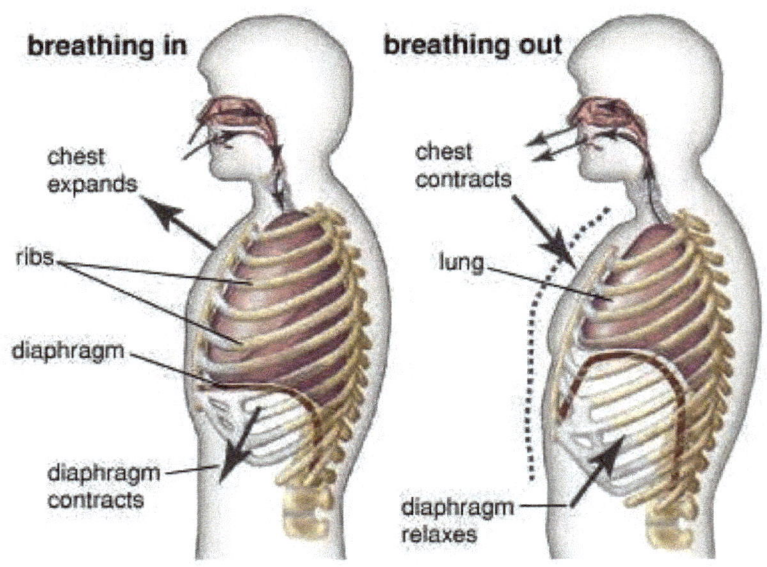

Air is draw into the right and left lungs by a muscular sheet that draws air into the lungs. This sheet is called a diaphragm that acts as a suction device. Raising the diaphragm experts pressure that causes waste-laden air to move out the same passages.

Benefits of Breathing

Breathing is one of the most vital operation, physiologically, speaking to sustain life. The benefit of deep breathing includes the following:
- Reducing blood pressure
- Increasing your energy levels
- Relaxing your muscles
- Improving the removal or elimination of waste
- Releasing endorphin of during pain relief
- Improving blood circulation
- Reducing sleeplessness
- Increasing focus in thinking or problem solving
- Helps in muscular flexibility

Incorrect breathing can cause exhaustion, vocal strain, more susceptibility to diseases or illnesses and increase in muscular aches.

Cardiopulmonary Resuscitation (CPR)

CPR is a lifesaving emergency procedure useful in some emergencies that includes heart attack and drowning. It is used to ensure the brain and heart continue to receive blood and function properly. When the heart stops, the lack of oxygenated blood can cause brain cells damages in only a few minutes. A person may die within eight to ten minutes from lack of oxygen. CPR keeps red oxygenated blood flowing to the brain and other vital organs.

It is better to do something than to do nothing at all if you are seeing someone in distress. It could mean someone's life or death. The American Heart Association recommends if you are untrained in CPR to use hands only. This means uninterrupted chest compression of 100 to 120 a minute until medical help arrive. You do no need to try rescue mouth to mouth breathing unless you are trained. This advice applies to adults, children and not newborns.

The Prophet Elijah was in a famine. There was no water in the streams. Elijah had no water to drink or food to eat (I Kings 17:3-6; 1 Kings 18:4). God told Elijah to go to a city, Zarephath. He would meet a woman there. The woman would give him food and water (1 Kings 17:7). Elijah met the woman. Her husband was dead. She lived with her son. Elijah asked her for some water and bread. She said she had only a little flour and oil to make bread for her son. Elijah told her to make some bread for him first. God would give her food until the famine was over. One day the woman's son became very sick. The sickness was so serious, that there was no breath left in him (1 Kings 17:17-20). Elijah was still living with the woman and her son at that time.

The son died in the bosom of the mother. Elijah took the dead body of the boy out of her bosom. Elijah carried him to the room where he was staying and laid the body on the bed. He prayed to God and then stretching himself upon the body three times. He prayed to God to let the child's soul come into him again. The boy was revived and Elijah took him to his mother who acknowledged that now she knew that he was a man of God (I Kings 17: 21-24).

This is the first documented account of life support method in the Bible. "And he went up, and lay upon the child (the soul and spirit had departed from the child (James 2:26), and put his mouth upon his mouth, and his eyes upon his eyes, and his hands upon his hands; and he stretched himself upon the child; and the flesh of the child of the Shunamite woman waxed warm.). The woman's son sneezed seven times and opened his eyes (2 Kings 4:34).

Just like Adam and Eve animals and plants also breathe to live. They can be called aerobic organisms. Humans and other organisms are aerobes. An aerobic organism or aerobe is an organism that can survive and grown in an oxygenated environment. Through cellular respiration organisms use oxygen to metabolize substances like sugars (glucose) or fats (lipids) to obtain energy called (ATP). Aerobic respiration has the advantage of yielding more energy than anaerobic respiration (little or no oxygen) called fermentation. An anaerobic organism is usually small like bacteria.

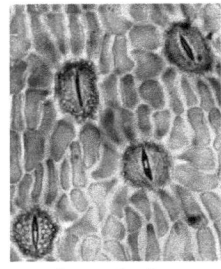 Transpiration: is the process by which moisture is carried through plants from root to small pores on the underside of leaves. Plants breathe through these very small openings in their leaves called stomata. Oxygen exit to the environment and carbon dioxide enter through these openings.

 Frogs breathes underwater through the skin. They can also on land breathe through their lungs.

Mountains-Through thermal expansion and contraction air moves in and out of spaces in rocks and rock release gases after periods of weathering and chemical decomposition. This might be stretching a little thin but could this be a form of breathing?

Bacteria can breathe but not like humans. They engage in the process of cellular respiration. Cellular respiration is the method by which cells convert chemicals into energy that the cell needs to stay alive.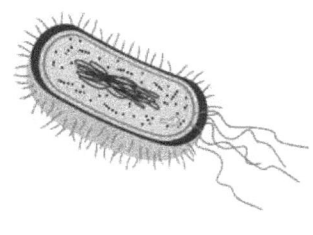

 **A fish b**reathes by taking water into its mouth and forcing it out through gills passages. As water passes over the thin walls of the gills, dissolved oxygen moves into the blood and travels to the fish's cells.

A **grasshopper** breathes through ten pairs of tiny holes called spiracles. Which are in the thorax and abdomen of the insect. Air enters the grasshopper's body through the front spiracles and exits through the rear.

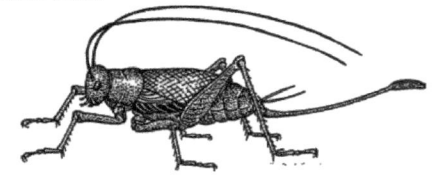

Respiration and a Baby's first cry

Babies first nine months after conception are spent in the mother's womb in an amniotic sac. They are not breathing in air in the womb but are receiving gaseous oxygen through the placenta and umbilical cord. Using a suction tube, after delivery the baby's doctor will clear the baby's mouth and nostrils of mucus and other fluids. The doctor does this to ensure that the baby's nostrils are clean and ready to take in oxygen. The baby should start crying
loudly if all air passageways are clear. The crying baby is a good sign of life because the lungs are now taking in air for the first time.

God breathe his own breath of life into man. "The spirit of God has made me, and the breath of the Almighty have given me life" (Job 33:4; Genesis 7:15, 22).

The Breath of God

The power of the breath of God is life giving (Genesis 2:7), altered nature (2 Samuel 22:16), change weather (Job 37:10), source of inspiration (2 Timothy 3:13-17), bring dry bones to life (Ezekiel 37:5), powerful force (Job 38:1), and the reception of the Holy Spirit (John 20:22; Acts 2:2).

Breathing reveals our complete dependence on God to sustain us from moment to moment. If you do not believe it just pinch your nose and hold it. Whew! Try this exercise of deep breathing: inhale and fill up your lungs with as much air as you can hold. As you inhale feel the air moving through your nose and into the lungs down to the bottom of your abdomen. Hold it. Count to ten. Now, exhale and release the air slowly. Feel your stomach muscles tighten as you exhale. Repeat this action a few times and note how you feel.

Always keep in mind that when you breathe the breath of God is flowing through you. God is with us (Isaiah 42:5; Psalm 104: 29-30).

Organization within Adam

Symmetry
The unifying concepts between Adam, Eve, and animals is the level of organization of their body in relationship to structure (anatomy) and functions (physiology). A quick reminder about symmetry. It is the body plan of the organism. The symmetry of an organism fits its lifestyle. Adam and Eve have bilateral symmetry in which their brain, sense organs, and mouth is in a distinct region, the head and not the knees. Other areas of their bodies; right and left sides; anterior end; posterior end, a back or dorsal surface and a bottom or ventral surface.

An example of bilateral symmetry in the Bible is the case of the wise King Solomon and two mothers. One day two women came to King Solomon, and one of them said: "Dear King, this woman and I live in the same house. Not long ago my baby was born at home, and three days later her baby was born. One night while we were all asleep, she rolled over on her baby, and he died. Then while I was still asleep, she got up and took my son out of my bed. She put him in her bed, then she put her dead baby next to me. In the morning when I got up to feed my son, I saw that he was dead. But when I looked at him in the light, I knew he wasn't my son. "No!" the other woman shouted. "He was your son. My baby is alive! The dead baby is yours." They argued back and forth in front of Solomon, until finally he said, "Both of you say this live baby is yours. Someone bring me a sword." A sword was brought, and Solomon ordered, "Cut the baby in half! That way each of you can have an equal part of him" (1King 3:16-27).

Framework

The 37th chapter of Ezekiel's vision give us insight from the Bible what happens to all body cells formed from mitosis into the arrangement or organization of tissues and organs in the human body. Also, we can consider this arrangement the possible creating action of Adams body plan and patterns.

"The Spirit of the Lord set me in the middle of a valley; it was full of bones. I saw a great many bones on the floor of the valley, bones that were very dry. He asked me, "Son of man, can these bones live?" I said, "Sovereign Lord, you alone know." Prophesy over those bones and say to them, "Dry bones, hear the world of the Lord! I will make breath enter you, and you will come to life. I will attach tendons to you and make flesh come upon you and cover you with skin; I will put breath in you, and you will come to life." And as I was prophesying, there was a noise, a rattling sound, and the bones came together, bone to bone. I looked, and tendons and flesh appeared on them and skin covered them, but there was no breath. I continued to speak and as he commanded me, and breath entered them; they came to life and stood up on their feet- a vast army" (Ezekiel 37:1-9).

"For you formed my inward parts; you knitted me together in my mother's womb. I praise you, for I am fearfully and wonderfully made. Wonderful are your works; my soul knows it very well.

My frame was not hidden from you, when I was being made in secret, intricately woven in the depths of the Earth. Your eyes saw my unformed substance; in your book were written, every one of them, the days that were formed for me, when yet there was none of them" (Psalm 139:13-16).

Below is the possible order of the arrangement of Adam in Genesis 2:7 and Ezekiel 37 of the human body as suggested in these passages:

- The dry bones or frame (Skeletal System)

- The sinews (a tough fibrous tissue uniting muscle to bone or bone to bone/tendons or ligaments)- (Muscular System and Connective tissues)

- The flesh upon the bones and sinews (Humans are composed of multiple cells. Cells come in many shapes and sizes depending on the function they perform. Cells with similar functions unite and form specialized tissues. The body contain four basic of tissues. They are muscles, connective, nerve, and epithelial tissues.

- The skin or other covering of flesh (Integumentary System)

- The breath of life (Respiratory System)

Bone of my Bone

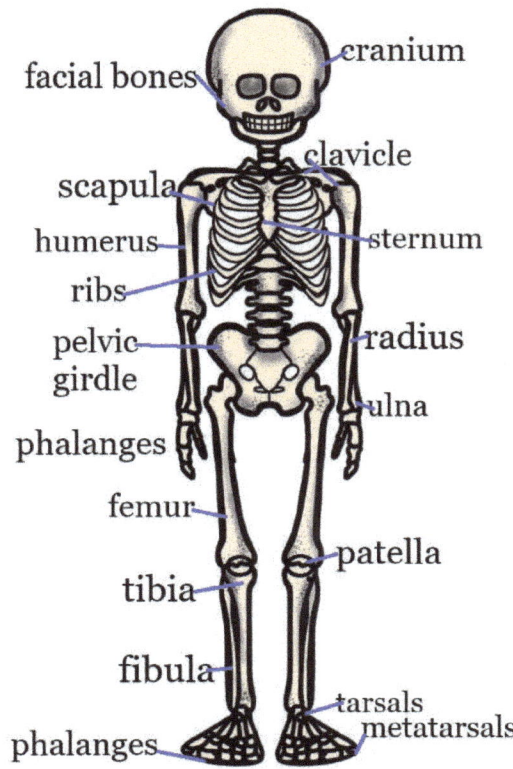

Adam received the breath of life through his nostrils. This action caused him to inhale and exhale air Oxygen). His newly formed body cells needed oxygen to function. As described earlier in this text the process of respiration began when the lungs were inflated. The circulatory, skeletal, and respiratory systems are all interconnected at this point. Let us start with the skeletal system and one specific set of long bones, the femurs. First what are the functions of the skeletal system:

- Serves as storage site for minerals like calcium and potassium that are essential for muscle contractions and controlling transmission of nerve impulse

- Site for fat shortage/yellow marrow- triglycerides for energy reserve

- Blood cells productions /red marrow

- Facilitation of movement – designs like lever system

- Site for attachment of muscles

- Protection of internal soft organs

- Growth in height on long bones
- Weight bearing capacity

The femur or thigh bone is the longest bone in the body and is used in walking, running, jumping and supporting variety of motions. The femur helps form the hip joint. It is the strongest bone in the body that bears the weight of the body. The femur is one of the sites where blood elements are formed.

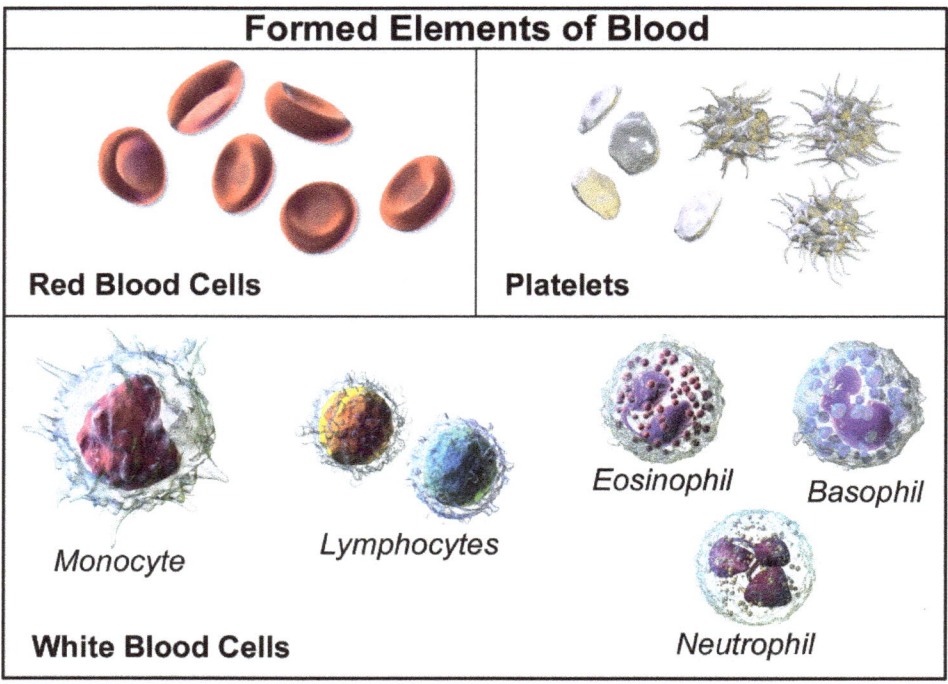

Blausen.com staff (2014)"Medical gallery of Blausen Medical 2014" *WikiJournal of Medic*

The blood is so vital to the body. "The blood is the river of life of the body" (Leviticus 17:11). Blood is composed of formed elements called red blood cells, white blood cells, platelets in suspended in fluid called plasma. The purpose of blood is:

- Oxygen supplier

- Immune system defender-detection of foreign material by antibodies

- Wound healer- clot formation

- Main transporter of nutrients- vitamins, sugar, and electrolytes

- Removal of waste materials- carbon dioxide, urea, lactic acids

- Maintain stable and constant body temperature
- Normalize pH level in tissues

- Hydraulic regulator- keep channel open for flow
- Messenger – transport hormones, enzymes to target cells

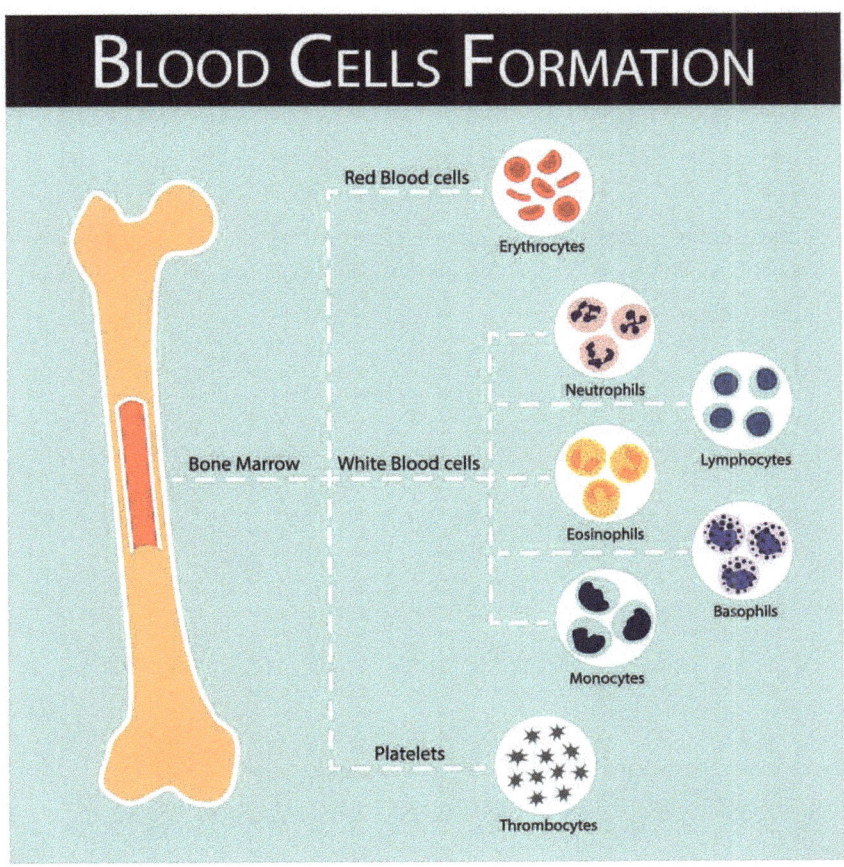

Next, the heart started pumping blood and messages were sent out that oxygen was low in this new body. A hormone produced in the kidney stimulates bone marrow to produce red blood cells, erythrocytes. This triggered a response in the bones. More Red blood cells are needed. The process by which blood cells are formed is called hematopoiesis (Latin: *hemato* = blood, *poiesis* = to make). Hematopoiesis formed the elements in blood. This takes place in the red bone marrow found in the end of long bones (humerus, femur), flat bones (ribs, cranial bones), vertebrae, and the pelvis.

-  Erythrocytes – Red Blood corpuscles. Non-rigid, concave shaped, sac of hemoglobin (a protein carrier of oxygen. RBCs picks up oxygen in the lungs and carrier oxygen to all the body tissues. Lifespan about 120 days.

- **Thrombocytes-** helps in blood coagulation/clotting. Lifespan of 10 days.

- **White Blood cell** – live a short life in the blood and connective tissue about hours to 4 days. They rapidly engulf foreign debris and elements

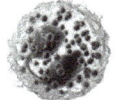

- *Eosinophil* -histamine release during allergic reactions
- - function in the immune system and release histamine, serotonin, and heparin

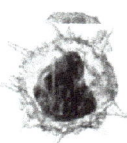

- critical in the functioning of the immune system that fight germs and clean up debris in wound healing

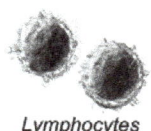

- reside in the blood and the lymphoid tissues (lymph nodes, spleen, thymus). Response to microorganisms and foreign bacteria, secretion of antibodies

Plasma is the liquid portion of the blood. It is made up of 92 % water and composed of proteins and salt solution. Now, the blood is flowing and reaching all tissues across the body. This will help make energy available for animation. Within the cells of the muscles (the flesh) are structures called mitochondria. The mitochondria supply energy in the form of ATP molecules. Mitochondria use the products of glucose in the presence of oxygen to break down into ATP.

Flesh of my Flesh-

The medical definition of flesh is considered the soft parts of the body o that is mainly composed 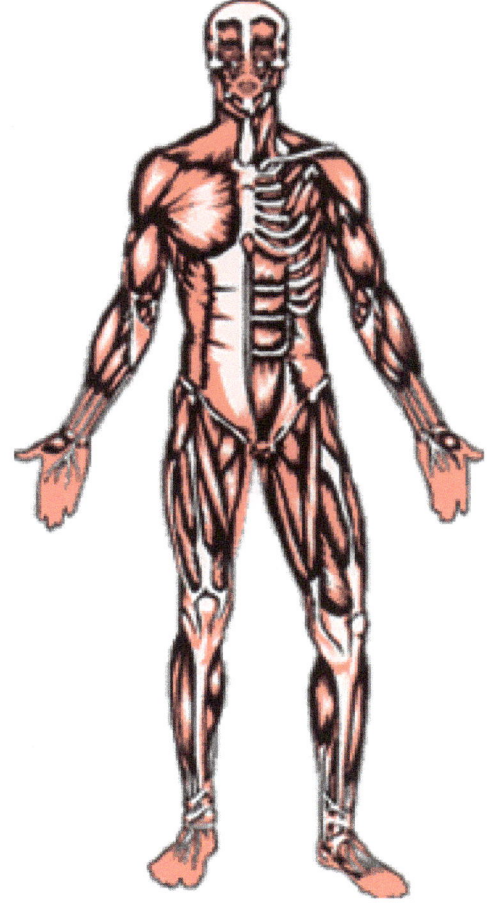 of skeletal muscles and fat that is found between the skin and bones of an animal or human. The Bible denotes flesh (Hebrews: *basar* and *seer*) in two ways. One meaning of flesh is the material of the outer body is mainly made of (Genesis 2:23; Matthew 16:17) and the other meaning is reference to the inner body (heart, soul) that which is contrary to the spirit and the desires of God. "For the sinful nature (the flesh) desires (lust) what is contrary to the Spirit, and the Spirit what is contrary to the sinful nature. They conflict with each other, so that you do not do what you want" (Galatians 5:17).

Muscles, the flesh, are the tissues in the body that have a high capacity to contract, extend, and become excitable which aid in producing movement. The body is made up of 640 muscles that help to maintain posture, generate heat and release waste products, breathing, shaping the body, controlling bodily functions such as eating, and comprises 40 % of your body mass. The three types of muscles tissue in our bodies are smooth (mainly in hollow organs and is controlled involuntarily– stomach), skeletal (muscles that are attached to the skeleton and can be controlled voluntarily), and cardiac muscle (found in the heart and is controlled involuntarily).

On average men have more muscle mass than women due to the male hormone called testosterone. Ligaments are connective tissues that attaches bone to bone. Tendons attaches muscles to bone allowing muscles to move the body

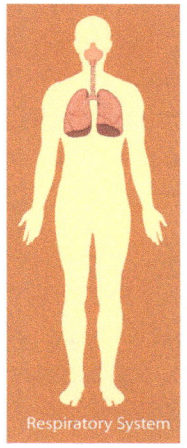
Respiratory System

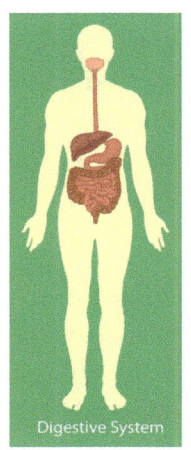
Digestive System

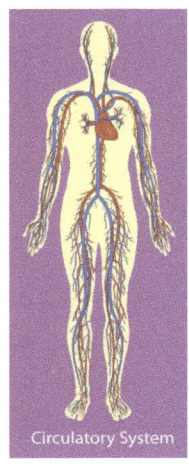
Circulatory System

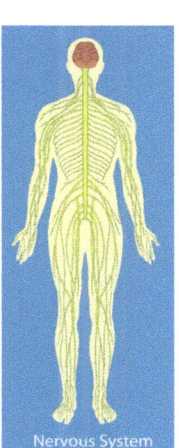
Nervous System

Eve -The Mother of All Living Things

Eve, the given name of the first woman means, "to live, life-giver, mother of all living things". Eve, the incredible living machine; the first woman; a wife; a mother; a grandmother. Eve was a perfect, innocent, sinless, and beautiful woman. Yet, she did become the world's first sinner. This first woman was created by a perfect God. She is the only woman in recorded history that had complete peace, lived in Paradise on Earth, and experienced all things being "very good".

Just like ourselves, she was composed of 60,000 miles of arteries, veins, blood vessels, racing all over her body supplying 100 trillion cells. Tissues, connective binding and lining tissues holding her together; 300 million tiny capillaries, 600 muscles, 5 million hair follicles over her body and 150,000 strands of hair in her natural crown on her head; 10 pints of blood pulsing through her vessels, and 206 muscles giving her feminine curves. Every human, give or take a little, have about the same physical makeup. Each of us have a pair of eyes, two lungs, thumbs, legs, and ears. We are all covered with skin and we breathe, all eat, digest, synthesize and assimilation of materials, and excrete waste. However, there were anatomical, physical and emotional components special only in the creation of Eve. This sets her apart from her husband, Adam. God blessed both Adam and Eve with different gifts that would enhance and complete each other.

Loneliness can be an unpleasant emotional response to isolation; comprising a of lack of communication, can be a mental health issue; bring on feeling of anxiety or incompleteness without personal companionship. God proclaimed it is not good for man (Adam) to be alone (Genesis 2: 18). He would need strength and support for the journey. God announced that he would make a helper suitable or companion after his own kind. An ezer, helper, suitable to man intellectually, morally, and physically. The glory and strength of Eve was deep inside of Adam.

Purpose of a Help-mate

Eve was formed out of purpose and function. The meaning of "help meet" stem from the Hebrew terms *ezer* and *k`enegdo*. The Hebrew terms have their meaning as 'to rescue', 'to save', 'to be strong' and 'salvation'. The Strong's Hebrew dictionary states "ezer" is "to surround, protect, or aid, succor." Meriam-Webster dictionary states the meaning of the word succor is someone that gives assistance and support in times of hardship and distress. A distinct kind of help. The expansion of the meaning of 'help meet' will add clarification and strengthen the position of women.

"And out of the ground the Lord God formed every beast of the field, and every fowl of the air; and brought them to Adam who was also formed out of the ground" (Genesis 2:19). The woman was unique in her creation in that she was only living organism what was formed in the Garden of Eden out of existing organic material. This organic material had regenerative properties that arise from a rib's bone marrow. Two new levels of technology were designed by the Creator. "And the Lord God caused a deep sleep to fall upon Adam, and he slept and he took one of his ribs, and closed up the flesh" (Genesis 2:21). God played a role of Chief Surgeon and his operating theater was the Garden of Eden. God administered the first anesthetic and performed the first surgery. Anesthetics are drugs used to prevent pain associated with surgery. These drugs work to block nerve transmission and to stop pain receptors sensations from reaching the brain. Anesthetics will affect several areas of the body. These areas include the brain waves, heart rate, salivary production, memory, your breathing, and muscle relaxation.

God took Adam and the animals out of the soil. However, woman was made from man. A biological and spiritual bond was now forged between them. Eve was not designed by God to be exactly like Adam, there are some unique differences.

XX Chromosome extraction

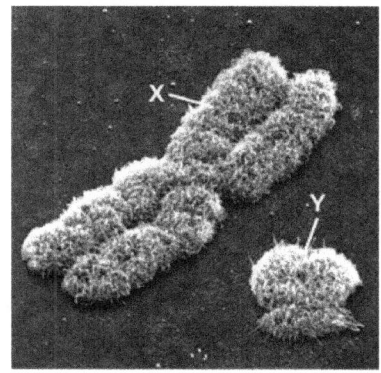

Adam and Eve are biologically, anatomically, endocrinologically, physiologically, and histologically exceptional creatures. Although both share similarities they both possess distinct differences. These differences prepared them for their roles in survival on Earth. Adam and Eve had difference chromosome profile. These differences are permanently imprinted in every cell of the body except for the gametes (the sex cells-egg, sperm). Human cells consist of 46 chromosomes which accounts for 23 pairs in each body cell. The first 22 pairs of chromosomes are called autosomes. The last pair, the 23rd, is called the sex chromosomes.

Eve's sex chromosomes profile is composed of two XX; while Adam chromosome pair is composed out a XY profile. The chromosome carries the genetic information that makes the difference between the genders. The female X chromosomes has more working genes that the male smaller 'Y' chromosomes. The 'Y' chromosomes give the organism its maleness.

Eve, a creation from Stem Cells

Ribs are truly amazing bones not only for the physical roles they play in our bodies, but also for their connection to Genesis. And the rib which the Lord God had taken from man, made a woman, and brought her unto the man (Genesis 2:22). Modern day science places this procedure under the area of medical biotechnology using adult stem cell therapy. Stems cells can differentiate into major cell types, tissues, organs, and eventually into a complete organism.

The process of adult stem cells therapy involves:

- Decide on a designated extraction site
- Preparation of the donor- use local anesthetics to be given by a certified physician
- An incision is made
- Stem cells are extracted from the bone
- Patient is sutured

- Rest, recovery, and healing time before patient is released

These amazing cells extracted from the bone marrow are called stem cells. Stem cells possess miraculous self-renewal potential when extracted from Adam. Stems cells have the potential to build other types of cells. Stems cells are present both before birth (embryonic stem cells) and in the adult body (adult stem cells).

Both men and women have 12 pairs of ribs. The ribs provide protection for the underlying organs, such as, the lungs and heart. The ribs form a protective cage around these very important organs. Second, they are one of the few bones that continue to make red marrow and blood cells in the adult. Third, the ribs serve as an attachment points for chest muscles involved in respiration.

Although all bones can repair themselves, ribs can regenerate themselves. Ribs are commonly removed during surgeries that require bone grafts in other parts of the body. The periosteum (membrane around the bone) must remain, as it contains osteoblast (bone making cells) which build the new rib bone. God chose a major bone that could regenerate itself in Adam physically and probably regenerate the missing ribs.

The stem cells from Adam's rib bone marrow would undergo cell division called mitosis and develop into other organized cell structures. These cells can develop into the four basic types of tissues: **epithelia** (provides an outer covering and boundary/the skin); **nerve** tissue (transmit electrical message from the brain to all body regions; **muscles** (contract and provide movement, shape, heat transmission); and **connective** tissue (bind, support, and hold things together).

Potential Application of Human Stem Cells

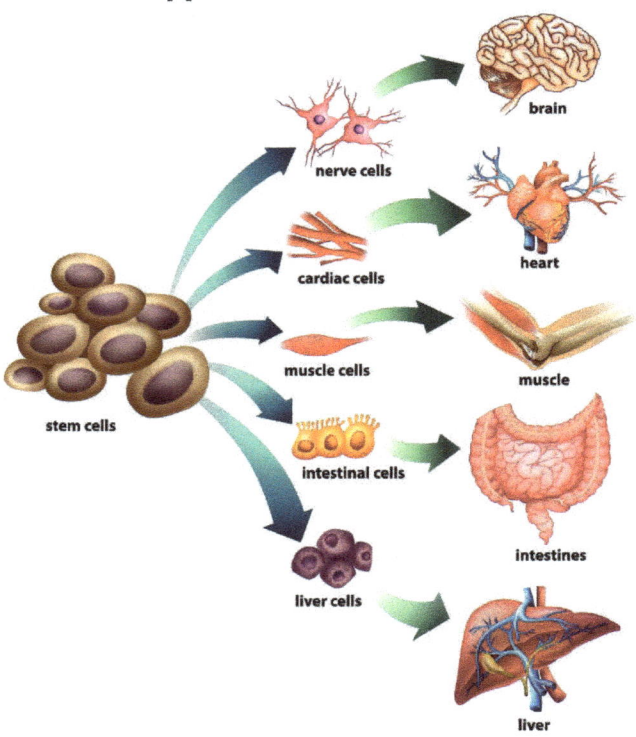

There is a little Eve in all of us

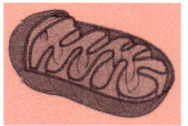 Mitochondria is a small double-membrane organelle floating freely throughout the cell functioning as the powerhouse of the cell. It gives the cell energy in a biochemical process that combine food (glucose) with oxygen to produce energy (ATP). This process is called cellular respiration. We can call it the batteries pack of the cells. The mitochondria are found in almost every cell in your body. Even animals and plants have these structures.

Most DNA is packaged in chromosomes within the nucleus, mitochondria also has a small amount of their own DNA. This genetic material is known as mitochondrial DNA or mtDNA. DNA or genes located in the nucleus get shuffled every generation. This is called recombination. Genetic recombination is the production of offspring with combination of traits that differ from those in either parent. However, mtDNA does not gets shuffled and recombination does not take place.

Every organism receives their mitochondria from their mother. This is made possible during the time of conception. Before conception mitochondria are located in the egg and the tail of the sperm. The sperms need vast amounts of energy to reach the egg for fertilization. Upon penetrating the egg cell membrane, the tail is seal off and sperm mitochondria does not become a part of the newly developing embryo. Thus, you have only the maternal mitochondria. A bit of Eve in all of us.

A mitochondrial DNA test traces a person's mother's line of ancestry using the DNA in his or her mitochondria. Basically, mtDNA is passed down by the mother unchanged to all her children, both male and female.

Hormones

The endocrine system controls the development of Eve's body. This system regulates growth, metabolism, reproductive processes, homeostasis, tissue development, sexual functions, and reproductive processes through hormones. These hormones bring on physiological responses in the body.

Chemical messages called hormones initiates and controls vital responsive in the body. These messengers are transported by the blood to specific target cells. Hormones are special bits of amino acids, peptides, secreted by the pea-sized pituitary gland. The pituitary gland is located at the base of the brain.

The pituitary gland release hormones to the male and female reproductive organs. The two main sex hormones are testosterone found in Adam (male hormone) and estrogen and progesterone in Eve (female hormones). Testosterone allowed Adam to have greater muscle mass, large bones, stronger ligament and tendons. His body could produce more red blood cells which was needed to delivery more oxygen to his massive muscles for work. (Genesis 2:8,15). This hormone also contributed to protein synthesis.

Estrogen and progesterone help to prepare Eve's body for pregnancy (Genesis 4:1-2, 25; 5:5); allows for secretion of osteoblasts (bone forming cells) that binds with calcium and Vitamin D;

helps the heart by relaxing blood vessels to increase blood flow; and help to keep the good cholesterol level high.

Eve's skeletal framework

Eve's skeleton or framework is not as massive as Adam. The three major differences in their skeletons are the size and shape of the ribcage, pelvis bones, and skull. Eve's chest is more rounded than Adam's. Eve's shoulder's widths are about the same but Adam has larger muscles groups and he appears to have wider shoulders. When Adam first saw Eve he proclaimed," Wow! This is now bone of my bone and flesh of my flesh" (Genesis 2:23). The lumbar curve is greater in women and her pelvis is tilted towards the front which made for the sway-backed appearance in Eve.

Eve's pelvis would be wider and more circular and adapted for gestation and for the passage of a baby during birth. Eve's hip was wider and influence the position of the femur, which are more angled than in men. This structural arranges give Eve a lightly "X" shaped frame. Women have looser ligaments. A woman would have a greater endurance or steady power to run a race while a man would have a great explosive power but fatigues more easily. Her ligament structure provided for greater flexibility in joints.

Eve developed more fat cells than Adam -Curves

Eve would have a higher subcutaneous (under the skin) fats than Adam. This serves as a reserve energy supply that will be used during pregnancy and gave Eve a round and curvy body. Fat in women is about 18%-20% higher than in men. Distribution of fat deposit on women could show up on the buttock, between the thighs, hips, pubis, knee, breasts, parts of the upper arms, or around the navel.

Women have smaller lungs and heart and this effects how they use oxygen. Women have a lower hemoglobin level and might be subject to greater incidents of iron-deficiency anemia.

Eve, the thinking woman's brain

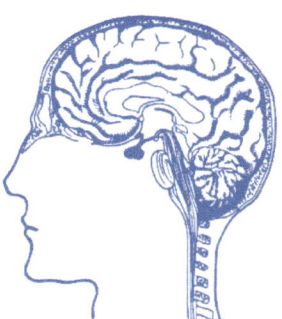

The master control center of the body is the brain. The brain keeps the body functioning smoothly. It is also the center of emotions and intellect. The brain assembles and interpret information received from the sense organs and the muscles. The brain is like a living computer composed of 100 billion nerve cells. The brain is about three pounds and is one of the most powerful organ controlling all activity of the body. It has a texture similar to firm jelly. The three main parts of the brain are cerebrum, cerebellum, and brain stem.

1. The **cerebrum** is involved in remembering, problem solving, thinking, feeling, and controls movement.
2. The **cerebellum** controls coordination and balance.
3. The **brain stem** connects the brain to the spinal cord and controls automatic functions such as breathing, digestion, heart rate and blood pressure.

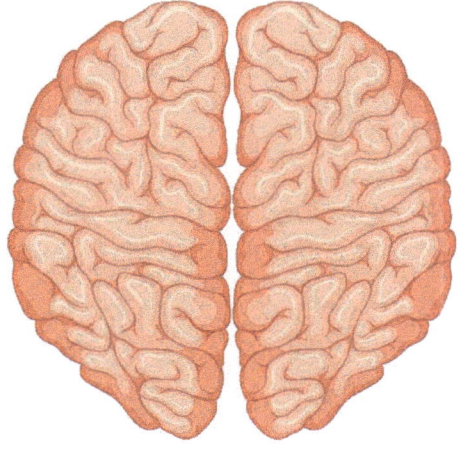

Left Hemisphere   **Right Hemisphere**

Language	Control the muscles on the left side of the body
Logical thinking	Comprehend visual imagery and make sense of what we see
Mathematical operation	Understanding concepts such as religion and philosophy
Detailed skeletal motor control	Creativity/imagination
Processing of fine visual and auditory details	Memory
Control the muscles on the right side of the body	Spatial relationship and patterns
Processing what you hear	Face recognition
	Non-verbal thinking

The brain is divided into two sides or hemispheres by the corpus callosum. Each side can be divided into four lobes: frontal, temporal, parietal, and occipital lobes. The corpus callosum sends motor and sensory functions back and forth between the right and left sides. This allows the brain to function seamlessly. Men generally are prone to be more left-brain strong. They approach problem solving from a task oriented perspective and women solve problems through feeling, communication, and creativity. When Eve and Adam eyes were open to the awareness that they were naked the run and hid (Genesis 3:7-10).

Scientists have discovered that they are actual structural differences between Adam and Eve brains. Certain parts or areas of their brain are different. Also, men and women think in a different way. The first record of a conversation between an animal and a human is Eve and the serpent. Eve listened and spoke to the serpent while Adam stood silently nearby (Genesis 3:1-6). Women tend to communicate more effectively than men. They talk through issues, express emotion, more sociable in groups. Men are more task oriented. Adam was given the assignment of tending the
Garden and Eden and naming the animals (Genesis 2:8). Men, also are less talkative. Men tend to process best in the left hemisphere while women tend to process equally between the right and left hemisphere.
In men the parietal lobe is a little larger in men on the left side. This section governs mental mathematical ability. The larger parietal lobe process sensory information on the right side in

women helps her to focus on actions, like her new born baby crying for milk (Genesis 4:1-2).

Men tend to have a "fight or flight" response as we see the couple hiding from God in the garden (Genesis 4:10-11).

Men and women perceive pain differently. She would vocalize her pain more than a man. She would also require more pain killer than men at the same level of pain. God proclaimed at judgement on Eve that she would have sorrow and pain that would be greatly multiply in conception and bring forth a child at birth (Genesis 3:16).

Lastly, the larger deep limbic system in the brain of women allow for more touchy-feely emotions which promotes bonding with others and the ability to serve as caregivers.

Relationship

These earliest ancestors, the progenitors of the human population (Genesis 1:26-27). "From one man (one blood) he made all the nations, that they should inhabit the whole Earth, and he marked out their appointed times in history and the boundaries of their land" (Acts 17:26). All human beings are related because they are descendent of the first man Adam and the first woman Eve (1 Corinthian 15:45).

This couple is first mentioned found in the book of beginnings, Genesis. Genesis speaks about the highlights of God, His creation and humankind in contact with creations and responses to other humankinds. Adam and Eve brought to the Earth the beginnings or laid the foundation of what does it mean to be part of human involvement.

A brief list of what Adam and Eve human experiences includes:

· Developing relationship and marriage (Genesis 2:18-24)

· Establishing the institution of family (Genesis 4:1-2; 4:25)

· Assignment of occupations and purposes (Genesis 2:15-20; Genesis 4:2-3)

· Formation of society and records of genealogy (Genesis 5:6-32)

· Eating (Genesis 2:16-17; Genesis3:6)

· Talking, Conversation, Communication (Genesis 3:2; Genesis 2:23; Genesis 3;4-5,13)

· Expression of emotions (Genesis 3:10-13; Genesis 4:6-8)

· Ecological mindedness of the Earth (Genesis1:3-25; Psalm 24:1)

· Decision making, asking questions, and critical thinking skills (Genesis 3:7,9)

· New technological process called surgery and the usage of existing organic material to create new organism (Genesis 2:21-22)

· Beginnings of worship, religious practice and offerings (Genesis 4-5)

· Developing and perfecting skills needed for developing civilizations arising from fertile gardens to curse land of thorns and thistles (Genesis 4:16-17)

· Open the portal for the entrance of sin into the new world (Genesis 3:7)

· Judgement or consequences of acts of disobedience (Genesis 3)

· Experiencing disappointments and pains (Genesis 3:24)

· Production of fabric as a covering of the body (Genesis 3:21)

· Promised Redeemer for all humankind (Genesis 3)

· Chronological time marker of the greater and lesser light (Genesis 1)

· Movement into history begins (Genesis 4-6)

The above experiences were catalysts at the grass-root levels of fundamental principles of **STEM** (science, technology, engineering, and mathematics). Adam and Eve were STEM-tastic! To be STEM-tastic involved awareness, acknowledgment, application and appreciation and apprehension of their environment.

Knowing your surrounding is relevant to your everyday survival. A scientist is a person, male or female, young or older engaged in systematic activities to acquire to acquire knowledge that describes and predicts the natural world. The term scientist was wordsmith or coined by the theologian, philosopher, and historian of science the Revered William Whewell (1794-1866). A scientist tries to understand how the world works, make observations, ask questions, find answers, share findings, establish patterns, and just figure things out.

Adam and Eve will be given the honorable position as the first scientists because it was essential for them to understand how the world worked. They had to make observations, ask each other questions, find answers, share findings, observe, and create patterns. STEM invades every aspect of their lives. They were the first to *Science* in the new world that included the rising and setting of the Sun, Moon, and Stars; land formations such as mountains, caves, valleys; rivers and water mist; diversity of animals and their life style; plants that covered the ground and trees that lifted the blue sky. *Technology* could include tools for agriculture to work the cursed ground of thorns, thistles, and weeds; simple machines like the wheel, wedge, lever, and the inclined planes. *Engineering* skills for building shelter, paving pathways, roads, and designing modes of transportation. Giving out portions and rations of food and provision; determining size and volume involved *Mathematics*.

Eve along with Adam were the early explores, scientists, and observers of their new environment. Eve experienced the first product of textiles and the origin of clothing. Clothing is fiber and textile materials worn on the body. Adam and Eve first sewed fig leaves and made temporary covering for themselves. The leaves they used to wrap themselves were probably were narrow and lack elasticity. The leaf fibers could not stretch to completely cover their bodies (Isaiah 28:20).

Garments of skins were made by God to clothe both (Genesis 3:21) after they became aware of their nakedness. Clothing was very important for this couple to survive. They were given covers to protect their bodies from heat, the cold, harsh wind, and other environmental exposures. The skins were most likely warm, strong, plain and coarse without embellishment or ornate colors. They were given, by God, as a pattern for this couple to continue to make and protect themselves from the harsh environment.

Adam and Eve appreciated the new clothing because they encountered hazardous activities of tilting and toiling the hard curse ground, thorns and weeds, insect bites, and rashes cause by plants. Clothing served as a hygiene barrier, protection from over exposure of ultraviolet radiation, and keeping infectious and toxic materials from direct contact with the skin.

The new couple is now in a strange and barren surrounding that required intense laboring, sweating, and aching muscles used for cultivation of the ground to be productive.

Educate to Innovate

"Science is more than a school subject or the periodic table, or the properties of waves. It is an approach to the world, a critical way to understand and explore and engage the world, and then have the capacity to change the world..." President Barack Obama, March 23, 2015

**Faith comes by hearing, Science comes by seeing.
What did Eve and the daughters of Eve see?**

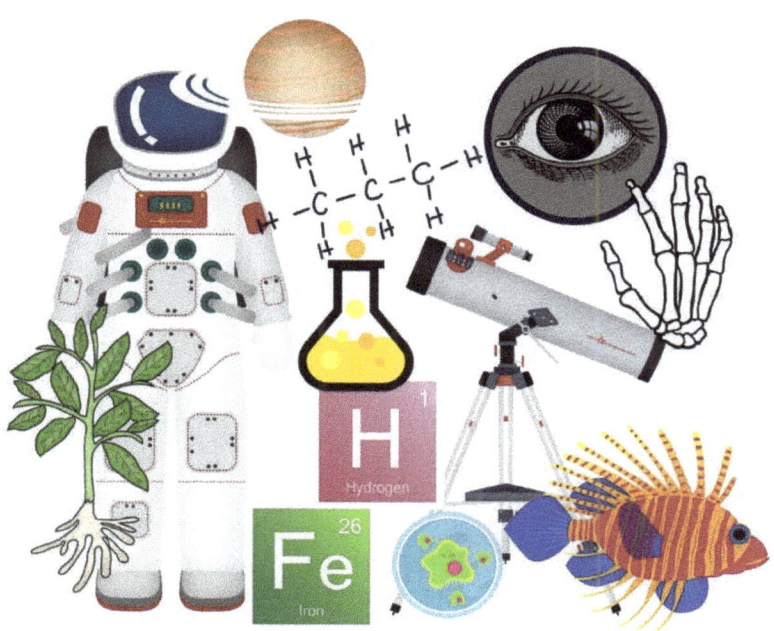

The Bible is an inspired text recorded by several authors from different backgrounds but with the same purpose of spreading the Good News. The Bible does not contain specific laws, principles and theories of science. The Bible contains an impressive range of varied dimensions of foundation information of early formal science. These dimensions included the pre-cursors in cosmology, astronomy, biology, medicine, botany, zoology, microbiology, physic, geology, ecology, and much more. Although the Bible is a book of faith, we can marvel at what can be revealed looking through the lens of faith using science as a scaffold to understand our environment.

A short list of some of the authors are Moses, Samuel, David, Solomon, Paul, and Luke. Many of the narratives they wrote about were witness first and in many case only by women. The information was later relayed to men or the community. Women on many occasions were not visibly noted as being present at key events in biblical history. However, they were there! Possible scenarios might include:

- Lot, Moses's nephew, two daughters were present when burning balls of sulfur rained down from the sky over Sodom and Gomorra (Genesis 19:20-24) or when their mother look back on the destruction of the cities and turned into a pillar of salt (Genesis 19:24).
- Noah's wife and three daughters-in-law saw the covenantal sign, after the world flood, of the rainbow in the sky (Genesis 9:12-17).
- The Himalayas mountains formed when India went crashing into Asia. Perhaps this happened during the time of Peleg, when the Earth was divided into continents (Genesis 10:25).
- Miriam, the leader of the women was among those who walk through the walls of the ocean created by the parting of the Red Sea and came out beating a hand-held percussion instrument, a tambourine.
- Mary Magdalen and the other Mary at the sepulcher listening to extraterrestrial intelligence beings called Angels (Matthew 28:1-7).
- Lastly, many skill women craft workers participated in making the priestly garments of gold, blue, purple, and scarlet yarns finely twisted linen (Exodus 28:6-14).

Women were industrialist as creator of products, imaginative, curious, intelligent, resourceful using available raw materials, problem solving, and observing daily phenomenal in nature. They were scientific thinkers.

The daily activities, survival skills, and responsibilities of women in a nomadic life style, as well as, nationhood led to an informal scientific method. Survival and thriving were essential to

managing challenges. Observation can be defined as the action of observing something or someone carefully to gain information. Women and girls gained information by carefully watching, listening, making inferences from things seen or experienced.

Today observations are referred to formally as the scientific method. This is an organized method to observe, discover, and record what is happening in your environment. This method consisted of several steps that includes problem, hypothesis, experiment, analysis and conclusion.

Technology and engineering was not abstract to biblical women. It is not a modern-day invention. Technology is the efforts to organize the world for problem solving so that goods and services can be invented, developed, produced, and used. It involves fulfilling a human purpose or need, using a method or a process, developing devices and tools to extract raw materials. The devices could be simple or complicated. The developed technology would affect or increase efficiency, resource, utensils, instruments, housing, clothing, transportation or weapons.

Through the centuries technology has become very vital to the development of civilization and easing the struggles of everyday human demands. Today, we are very comfortable and dependent on technological devices that sets the television through remote control for sleeping, texting message on cell phone through invisible wires or transportation across the nation in the air in hours.

The people during Bible times used simple and compound machines. Machines help to make work easier like pushing, pulling, and lifting heavy objects. A simple machine is something that changes the direction of the force or the amount of force required to move an object. Simple machines that women used were levers (using rods to lift heavy load without pushing very hard); pulleys rope and pails to lift water from wells; wheels used for transportation to move things; screw for grinding grains; and inclined planes (a ramp) used to move thing from a lower place to a high place and reverse. The Bible reveals that ancient women had jobs and careers that involved the use of simple machine (Proverbs 31) They used looms, wheel and axles, spinning wheel, weaving, plough, daggers, sling, spears, and javelins The Bible mentions women working in agriculture (Ruth 2:8), millers (Matthew 24:41), as perfumers and cooks (1 Samuel 8:13), shepherds (Genesis 29:9); textiles crafters (Acts 18:3); and midwives (Exodus 1:15).

Conclusion: STEM Education Matters

"Science is now saying what the Bible has said for thousands of years:
that at the beginning of time there was a day without a yesterday"- womeninthebible.net

In conclusion, STEM (Science, Technology, Engineering, Mathematics) education is important to humanity's global future that shapes our daily experiences. Science is what we see in our natural world – the Sun, Moon, Stars, wind, botanical, zoological and microscopic life, water, land, mountains shaking, and food. This first series of *Faith comes through Hearing. Science comes through Seeing: New Beginnings* integrates faith and science. This series also reveals the Bible as an essential study guide we can trust. The Bible helps us to grasp the basics of life through our faith and science.

Humanity has discovered new knowledge and has accomplished great feats. "There is nothing new under the Sun "(Ecclesiastes 1:9) refers to what is happening on Earth since the beginning of time. Humans can be likened unto the laws of nature. Our thoughts, actions, behaviors are recycling over time What which has been will be again. What is new is the methodology of how things are done. Humanity has a desire to know. Our knowledge base comes through observations developed into applications through history, prophecy, laws, poetry, the arts, literature and foundational building blocks of scientific foreknowledge.

Science cannot be placed over the Scripture. The Scripture is the authoritative, irrevocable, inspired Word of God and the role of His Son (John 1:1-4; Colossians 1:16). The Scripture is about real people in real places with real problems seeking solutions and acknowledging through thanks and praises their dependence on God. God wants us to know Him and provided us with greater understandings of His glory through science, as the Great Designer and Creator of all. "Your knowledge is beyond my comprehension. It is so far beyond me. I am not able to fathom it" (Psalm 139:6; Romans 11:33).

Science is observable and can be fallible. Science must be tested repeatedly over time to prove or maintain its factuality and integrity. However, when new evidence is presented with the new knowledge the position of science produces a new voice and changes. The Word of God is eternal and constant from generation to the next generation. "Heaven and Earth may pass away but my word never fails" (Matthew 24:35). It tells us how God had a logical plan described in Genesis 1-3 that gave us the origins of time, space, matter, and redemption. His plan involved creation with an awesome regenerative sustainable energy source. This energy source, the Holy Spirit, united simple elements into complex molecules and compounds that formed simple celled life forms in a chemical soup over billions or millions of years ago. These frames of time are woven throughout the Bible narratives and civilization. Our belief and acceptance of these narratives is by faith (Hebrews 11:3).

Technology is the application of scientific knowledge. It brings about development of a piece of equipment, a method, and machinery. Technology is also using science to invent useful thing to use to solve problems. Technology science of craft (Greek *techne*- art, skill cunning hands; *logia*- collection of skills, processes, methods. Technology can be used in war tools, building structures, equipment, and worship.

The first evidence of technology in the Bible is when Adam and Eve took fig leaves to produce clothing (Genesis 3:7,21). Other use of technology is Noah building the Ark (Genesis 6-8); Tower of Babel (Genesis 11:4); making musical instruments (1 Samuel 18:6, Nehemiah 12:36); building an Altar (Exodus 20:24-25); double-edge sword (Hebrews 4:12); war equipment (Joel 3:10) and a lamp (Psalm 119:105).

Engineering is the branch of science concerned with the design, construction of building, launching ships, bridges, and use of engines. Examples of civil engineering starts with Cain, the first son of Eve, in building the city of Enoch (Genesis 4;17-18); highways (Isaiah 19:23); improving mode of transportation on streets (Zechariah 8:4-5); Road to Damascus (Acts 9:1-19) rebuilding cities (Ezekiel 36:33-36).

Mathematics is about numbers, quantity, and space. Illustrations of math include the incident of counting fishes (John 21:11); measuring line (Zechariah 2:1-2); counting the number of hairs on your head (Matthew 10:30); multiplication (Genesis 6:19-20); count the cost (Luke 14:28); and Ark measurements (Genesis 6:15-16); period of a day (Psalm 90:12).
Women played a versatile role as early scientists. Starting with the mother of all living things, Eve, started the spiral stairways to obtaining knowledge. Eve and the daughters of Eve, that followed her most likely initiated the use of 'doing science 'first in their gardens and their kitchens. As early nomads they needed to observe and survive in their environment. They made and used pottery, basketry, metal blades, used hearths, bio fuels, use of medicinal plants (herbs)ground grains, season with herbs, fermentations of cheese and wines, roasting, use leaven for yeast cells and added condiments (salts, vinegars, oils).

Eve and the daughters of Eve used creativity, curiosity, observation, motivation, and innovation to address the critical demand placed on them from sin. Access to new knowledge and practices are treasured in the Bible. Spending effectual and fervent study time of passages and narratives will enrich our awareness of nature that leads to the Creator.

STUDY GUIDE

SCIENCE
FAITH
TENDONS
LIGAMENTS
MUSCLES
THERMODYNAMIC
TECHNOLOGY

CHAPTER 1: THE BIBLE IS NOT A SCIENCE BOOK BUT…

1. "Test all things hold fast what is good."
2. Science emerges through the Scriptures

CHAPTER 2: DISCOVERY SCIENCE

1. Biblical Women were technologically skilled
2. Personal connections to Faith and Science
3. The Chemistry of Baking a Cake with Grandma Sarah
4. Grandma's Hands
5. Science behind a Woodstove- Thermodynamic
6. Grandma's Peete's Loving Hands- tendons and muscles working together
7. Let's cook Biscuits

1. What lesson(s) have you learnt from someone of a different generation than yours?
2. State your personal definition of science.
3. Write your personal proclamation of your faith or belief.
4. Can science and religion coexist in harmony? Why or Why not?
5. Have you taken any lessons in science in school that challenged your religious belief? How did you deal with it?
6. Read Daniel 1:4. Why would the understanding of science be important to the Hebrew boys in Babylon?
7. If someone ask you the question," What is your proof for the existence of God?" What might you answer?

SCIENTIFIC METHOD
OBSERVATION
THEORY
CREATION
EVOLUTION
ANGEL

CHAPTER 3: SEARCHING THE SCRIPTURES

1. Faith comes by Hearing. Science comes by Seeing. What did they see?
2. In the Beginning God Created
3. Abracadabra: Creating Nothingness into Something
4. Celestial Beings or Extraterrestrial Messengers

1. Science lessons are designed to equip students with critical thinking skills. Tell how the scriptures has inspired you to ask or seek evidence for claims of truth as a critical thinking believer?
2. How might you deal with an awkward situation that contradicts your religious belief? For example, "the theory of evolution" (change over time in a population of an organism) versus creation.
3. What are angels?
4. How are angels important to God?
5. How are angels important to humanity?
6. Who is Lucifer?
7. Describe the physical attributes of Lucifer.

| PNEUMATOLOGY POWER ENERGY GEOLOGY | **CHAPTER 4: UNQUENCHABLE ENERGY ON THE MOVE**

1. Cosmic time- Big Bang or the Big Bam
2. Magi Reading the signs in the sky
3. Big Bang-Age of Radiation
4. Property of Visual Light
5. Earth's Geological time scale
6. How did water come to Earth?
7. Our world dark with emptiness
8. The effects of the impact
9. What happened during the impact? | 1. Define: unquenchable. How can this definition apply to the power of the Holy Spirit?
2. "Even though we cannot see the Holy Spirit, he is present around us just like the wind. And just like the wind pushes a leaf through the air, the Holy spirit guides us through life." www.thereligiousteacher.com. Read Acts 2:2 and what connection can you discover between the Holy Spirit and wind?
3. Discover the attributes of the Holy Spirit
   a. Intelligence-1 Cor. 2:10-13
   b. Has feelings – Ephesians 4:30
   c. Has a will – 1 Cor 2:11
   d. Prays- Romans 8:26
   e. Does miracles – Acts 8:39
   f. Teaches us – John 14:26
   g. Reminds us of prophecy – John 16:13
4. What did the Holy Spirit do during creation (Genesis 1:2; Job 33:4; Genesis 2:7)?
5. List the gifts of the Spirit mentioned in Isaiah 11:1-3?
6. The word power in Greek is 'dunamis' from which we derive the English word dynamic. What is the meaning of the Greek word 'dunamis' in the following passages:
   a. Mark 9:1
   b. Matthew 25:14-30
   c. Luke 5:17
   d. Luke 4:36 |
| DYNAMITE EXPLOSION | **CHAPTER 5: EARTH'S NUCLEAR WINTER**

1. Trouble in Heaven
2. Names of Satan
3. Speed of Angels | 1. What happened that the angel called Lucifer went through a name change to Satan?
2. List the character of Satan after reading the following passages:
   a. Ezekiel 11-17; Matthew 13:28
   b. John 8:44
   c. Matthew 13:39
   d. 1 Peter 5:8-9
   e. Isaiah 14:12
   f. Matthew 4:1-11
   g. James 4:7
3. In scripture Satan is compared to the following:
   a. Psalm 91:3
   b. Matthew 13:4
   c. John 10:10-12
   d. 1 Peter 5:8-9; Rev. 12:3-12
4. What comfort can you find in these passages: Mt.8:16-17; Mk.16:17; Luke 10:17? |

CREATION
METEOROLOGY
ASTRONOMY
OCEANOGRAPHY
CURRENTS

CHAPTER 6: REVIEW, RESTORE, REPLENISH

DAY ONE - SETTING OFF SPIRITUAL DYNAMITE

1. Nuclear Winter
2. Brooding and Hovering over the Deep
3. The Ocean and mixing Primordial Soup
4. God speaks- It happens!
5. Conversations with Taking Animals
6. God Puffs into Adam
7. Time began--Let there be light

DAY TWO: RESTORATION OF THE HEAVENS

1. The Atmosphere
2. Fluffy White Clouds

DAY ONE

1. The Earth had historically gone through many phases. Describe the condition of the Earth in Genesis 1:2.
2. What can we discover about the dateless past from the scriptures. Read pages Proverbs 8:22-26; John 1:1; Hebrews 11:3.
3. Read Job 38:4-7 to discover what was created first.
4. God commanded action from the universe. Read Genesis 1:3 and write that statement.
5. Find the rotational speed of the Earth on its axis.
6. Find the tilt of the Earth's axis.
7. Describe the length of a period called a day - Genesis 1:4.
8. Where do you find the concepts of time, space, and matter in the following verse Genesis 1:1?
9. The Spirit of God moved on the deep. This science has been described like a "mother hen hovering or brooding over her egg". What insight can this metaphor be used to describe the power of the Holy Spirit?
10. The Holy Spirit is the power of God: Titus 3:5-6; John 20:22; Acts 2:4; and Acts 10:39.
11. How does science explain what is light?
12. The Earth was dark in Genesis 1:1a. How long does it take for light to travel from the Sun to the Earth?

DAY TWO

1. Write the following divine commands that started with the phrase, "And God said," from Genesis 1:3-29.
2. Define the term firmament. How is it described in Isaiah 40:22 and Jeremiah 10:12?
3. "And God called the firmament Heaven." This is portion of the sky is called the first heaven. Read Genesis 1:20 and state what happens in this atmospheric level.
4. What types of forces might be needed to divide or separate something?
5. Describe the first two division made by God in Genesis 1:4 and Genesis 1:7.
6. Find the functions or role of clouds in the atmosphere:
    a. Judge 5:4
    b. Exodus 13: 21-22
    c. 2 Chronicles 5:13-14
    d. Acts 1:9; Luke 21:29
    e. 1 Thessalonians 4:17
7. Wind is created by heating molecules in the atmosphere:
    a. East wind- Genesis 41:6; Exodus 10:13; Jonah 4:8
    b. South wind- Job 37:17; Psalms 78:26; John 12:55
    c. North wind- Proverbs 25:23; Ecclesiastes 1:6

PLATE
TECTONIC
EARTHQUAKES
GERMINATION
FERTILIZATION
POLLEN
SEEDS
GEOLOGY
BOTANY

DAY THREE: RESTORATION OF THE SEAS AND THE LAND

1. Important properties of water
2. Meteorological Phenomena- effects of water on the Earth's surface and atmosphere
3. Start of the longest rain recorded in the Bible
4. Shaking and Quaking from Fault lines
5. Surveying the Land Forms
6. Colonization of the Land
    a. Importance of Plants
    b. Plant diversity
    c. Seeds
    d. Herbs
    e. Grasses
    f. Flowers
    g. Fruit production
    h. Trees

1. God created the first three life form connected to the water and the land. Read Genesis 1:11-12 and name them.
2. God formed the ocean basins and the continental land masses. What is Pangea?
3. What happened to the large land mass mentioned in Genesis 10:25?
4. Describe the science of plate tectonic?
5. What is a seed? What is a fruit
6. What are the states of seed germination?
7. How are herbs beneficial to animals and humans?
8. Why are flowers significant to the production of food?
9. Make a list of different types of trees mentioned in the Bible:
    a. Chestnut- Ezekiel 31:8
    b. Cedar 1 King 4:33
    c. Oak – Isaiah 6:13
    d. Hazel- Genesis 30:37
    e. Mulberry – 2 Samuel 5:23
    f. Olive – Deuteronomy 24:20
    g. Pomegranate – 1 Samuel 14:2

ROTATION REVOLUTION LUMINARIES NUCLEAR FUSION SOLAR FAMILY STARS SUN EARTH LIGHT	**DAY FOUR: LIGHTS IN THE GREAT SKY** 1. Earth's yellow star: The Sun 2. The Moon 3. Twinkle, Twinkle little Star	1. What is the name of the two great light holders or luminaries in the sky? Genesis 1:14 2. State the key functions of these two great lights. Genesis 1:14-18 3. Compare the Earth's rotation to the Earth's revolution. 4. What is the period of movement of the Earth and the Sun? The Earth and the Moon. 5. Stars are another source of light in the night sky. Find out why Stars appear fixed against night sky. 6. Why do Stars appear to twinkle? 7. Read the following passages to extract information about the Solaris Covenant: Genesis 8:22; Psalm 89: 34-37; Jeremiah 31:35-37. 8. Name a few of the actions of the Sun: Isaiah 38:8; Luke 4:40; Genesis 15:12, 17; Numbers 2:3 9. What is the source of Moonlight? 10. What is the light source of the Sun and Stars?
TAXONOMY BINOMIAL - NAMING SYSTEM ANIMALS ZOOLOGY MICROORGANISMS	**DAY FIVE: ANIMAL- CREEPING, CRAWLING, FLYING, LEAPING, SWIMMING THINGS** 1. Division of living things into kingdoms 2. Micro-organism: It's a small world after all 3. God loves animals and He blessed them 4. Animals as our first teachers 5. Animals used in miraculous ways Survey of the Animal Kingdom	1. The creation of flying insects, fungi, bacteria are not mention in the creation story. Tell what types of animals were recorded in Genesis 1:20-23. (Remember the creation story is a brief condense account of what happened). 2. Write out John 1:3. What does it mean to you? 3. Give examples of swarming and creeping things: Genesis 7:21; Leviticus 5:2,11,20,21; Deuteronomy 14:19. 4. Distinguish between 'made' and 'create'. 5. What type of animal is mentioned in Matthew 12:40? 6. Read about the great fish and Jonah (Jonah 1:15-2:1). 7. After God blessed the animal (Genesis 1:22) what did He command then to do? 8. What does it mean "after your own kind" – Genesis 1:24-25? 9. Adam was the first taxonomist. What did he do?

DUST
DIRT
LITHOSPHERE
AEROBIC RESPIRATION
ANAEROBIC BREATHING
BLOOD
CHROMOSOMES
STEM CELLS
ANIMALS
SYMMETRY

DAY SIX: LARGE ANIMALS AND HUMANITY CREATED

1. Volcanic eruption: The source of dust
2. Atmospheric circulation and distribution of soil
3. The color of soil
4. Establishing the foundation for life
5. Animal Kingdom survey

II. *The Adam Experience*
1. The Puff- Respiration
2. Cardiopulmonary Resuscitation - CPR
3. Organization with Adam
    a. Symmetry
    b. Framework
    c. Blood
    d. Muscles and Organs Systems

III. **Eve- the mother of all living beings**
   a. Purpose of a Help-mate
   b. X-chromosome extraction
   c. Eve: a creation from Stem Cells
   d. There is a little Eve in all of us
        i. Hormones
        ii. Eve's skeletal framework
        iii. Eve developed more fat cells than Adam
        iv. Eve the thinking woman's brain
   e. Relationship

5. STEM
6. Educate to Innovate

1. What is dust? What are atoms?
2. Define the following terms: inorganic, organic, abiotic, biotic, elements.
3. What is respiration? How did God respire Adam?
4. What is a template? How is Adam is the original template of humankind?
5. Describe the symmetry of humans.
6. The levels of organization of multicellular organism are cell, tissue, organ, system, and organism. Define each level.
7. What are stem cells?
8. Eve is described as Adam's helpmate. What things might Eve do to help Adam?
9. Describe the elements of a good relationship.
10. Why is STEM (science, technology, engineering, and mathematics) education so important for everyone?

References

Chapter 1: Kitchen Science

Arthur, Meredith; Slatkin Eric, Smith; Blake. Kwanzaa cooking with Grandma Martha. YouTube (2010)

Begley, Sharon, *Science Finds God.* (July 20,1998). Newsweek. vol.132, No. 3, p. 46-51

Di Christiana, Mariettle. (July 22,2014). Why Science Is Important. Scientific America. Retrieved from https://www.scientificamerican.com/article/why-science-is-important

en.wikipedia.org/wiki/define scientist

Islam, Celia. Closing the stem gender gap: Why is it importance and what can you do to help? (January 23, 2014). Retrieved from https://www.huffingtonpost.com/celia-islam/closing-the-stem-gender-g_b_3779893.html

Kellogg, E. E. Science in the kitchen. Kindle ed. (May 3,2004)

Smith, Sarah Rae. Leaveners and Fats. The Science of Great Biscuits. (February 22, 2010). Retrieved from https://www.thekitchn.com/leaveners-fats-the-science-of-109416

Wolke, Robert L. What Einstein told his cook: Kitchen Science explained. Kindle ed. (2008)

www.scienceofcooking.com

Chapter 2: Sacred Writing

Davis, Denise. When Jesus Speaks, Things Happen!www.iwrite4HIM.com

Finis Jennings Dake Annotated Bible

Wellman, Jack. What do Angels look like A Biblical Analysis. (July 4, 2011). Retrieved from www.whatachristianswanttoknow.com

Wellman, Jack. What do angels look like: A Biblical Analysis? Retrieved by www.whatchristianswanttoknow.com/ (07/4/2011)

www.biblehub.org

www.gotquestions.org/attributes-God.html

Chapter 3: Energy on the Move

Carnegie Mellon University. Science notes: Chemical Formation. Retrieved from

Easton's Bible Dictionary: Power (dunamis)

God Repairs the Earth. www.thereluctantmessenger.com

Got Question Ministries. What names and titles does the Bible use for the Holy Spirit? Retrieved from https://www.compellingtruth.org/names-Holy-Spirit.html . (2011)

http://geologycafe.com/oceans

http://www.chem4kids.com/glossary.

http://www.physicsclassroom.com

Kenny, James. A history of life on Earth: the Precambrian Era. Retrieved from

Greene, Brian. How did water come to the Earth? Retrieved from www.smithsonianmag.com/ (May, 2013)

LaHaye, Tim; Hindson, Ed. (2004) The popular encyclopedia of Bible Prophecy. Oregon Harvest House Publishers.

Marshall, Scoot Dr. Cosmology and the Birth of the Earth. Retrieved from http://www.appstate.edu/~marshallst/GLY1101/lectures/1Formation_Of_Universe.pdf (2017)

Minderhoud:, Joel .The Nitrogen Cycle: Upheld and governed by God (February 1, 2004). Retrieved from .https://standardbearer.rfpa.org/articles/

Origin of the Earth's atmosphere Retrieved from http://www.ux1.eiu.edu/~cfjps/1400/atmos_origin.html

UCAR Center for Science Education. How volcanoes influence climate. Retrieved from https://scied.ucar.edu/shortcontent/how-volcanoes-influence-climate

Woodward, Kenneth L. How the Heavens Go. Newsweek. vol.132, No.3, 1998, p.51

Chapter 4: The Little Big Bang

Brent L. *(1992),* "War in Heaven", *in* Ludlow, Daniel H, Encyclopedia of Mormonism, *New York:* Macmillan Publishing, pp. 1546–1547,

Gap Theory and/or The Ruin and Reconstruction: Theory of Genesis 1. Retrieved from www.thereluctantmessenger.com

Hartmann, William K. The impact that wiped out the dinosaurs. Retrieved from https://www.psi.edu/

Line, Brent. Asteroid impacts: 10 biggest known hits. Retrieved from https://news.nationalgeographic.com/news/2013/13/130214-biggest-asteroid-impacts-meteorites-space- (February 15, 2013)

Chapter 5: Renew, Restore, Replenish: Day One to Five

Blank, Wayne. Trees of the Holy Land. Daily Bible Study. Retrieved from www.keuway.ca

Deem, Rich The human difference: How humans are unique compared to all other animals. Retrieved from http://www.godandscience.org/evolution/imageofgod.html

Dewey J. F. (1972). Plate Tectonics. Scientific America. v.226, p. 56-68

Duke, Jim. Biblical Botany. www.biblicalgarden.com/Plants

Elwell, Walter A. Baker's Evangelical Dictionary of Biblical Theology

Gillen, Alan Dr. Microbes and the days of creation. (January 16, 2008) Retrieved from https://answersingenesis.org/days-of-creation/microbes-and-the-days-of-creation/

Hennigan, Tom; Bergman, Jerry. The Origin of Trees. www.creationsearch.org

Hepper, Nigel. Plants in the Bible. www.biblicalgarden.com/Plants

http://www.icr.org/article/continental-drift-plate-tectonics-bible -by Stuart E. Nevins, M.S.

Javor, George T. The Bible and Microbiology. (March 15, 2004). Retrieved from http://adventist.org/essays/

Musselman, L. J. Dr. All the plants of the Bible. www.biblicalgarden.com/Plants

noaa.gov

Temple, Joe. Aaron's Rod. The Pulpit Commentary:

Understanding the Moon phases. www.moonconnection.com

www.biblestudytools.com

www.climatekid.nasa.gov/ocean

www.eniscuola.net

www.genesisandgenetics.org/genetics-of-kinds.pdf

www.physicsclassroom.com/blueskies

www.sciencedaily.com/originoflife

www.thebrookenetwork.org

www.Truebiblecode.com

www.volcanology.geol.uscb.edu: Soil from volcanoes

Chapter 6: Day Six

Blank, Wayne. Daily Bible Study by: Leviticus 13: Bacteria

Bushnell, Katherine C. God's Word to Women: One Hundred Bible studies on Women's place in the divine economy (God's Word to Women Publishers: 1923, 1988,1998), 32-34

Catholic Encyclopedia: Eve

Darwish, Hisham. The male brain versus the female-brain-the anatomical differences: https://thinkmarketingmagazine.com/

Delavier, Frederic. Skeletal differences between women and men. Why woman carry more fat than men. Excerpts from Women's strength training anatomy. Retrieved from http://humankinetics.com.excerpts on 9/27/2017

Heather. The real meaning of the term "helpmeet Retrieved from www.womeninthescriptures.com., (November 9,2010)

Hensley, Amber. Big difference between men's and women's brains www.mastersofhealthcare.com/blog/2009 10

http://www.sciencenewsforkids.org/articles/20051019/Feature1.asp
Lanza, Robert et al. Essentials of stem cell biology. Amsterdam. Boston, Elsevier, 2006. p. 548

Masterson, Kathleen. From Grunting to Gabbing Why humans can talk. – audio transcript

Meador, Jon. Why God used Adam's Rib to create Eve. Retrieved from https://www.gotquestions.org/Adams-rib.html (May 1, 2010)

Orr, James, M.A., D. D. Generator Editor. "Entry for 'Flesh". "International Standard Bible Encyclopedia". 1915

Purdom, Georgia Dr. The Amazing Regenerating Rib. Retrieved from http://www.vananne.com/serpentdove/The%20Amazing%20Regenerating%20Rib.htm.(February 4, 2009)

Sohn, Emily. From stem cell to any cell. (Oct. 19, 2005). Science News for Kids. The Human Race: Its creation, history, and destiny: The creation of Man. www.bible.org

The Woman of Unique Distinction-Eve. www.biblegatesay.com/resources/all-women-bible/Eve

Towns, Elmer L. (2003). Bible Answers for almost all your questions. Thomas Nelson

What are stem cells? (Everybody Mysteries: Fun Science Facts from the Library of Congress

What are stem cells? (Everybody Mysteries: Fun Science Facts from the Library of Congress

Photo & Illustrations Credits
Openclipart.org
Front Cover: Canstock>com
https?www.bing.com/public domain image

U.S. Department of the Interior U.S. Geological Surveys (USGS)

Pink flower & butterfly-Ang Kim
Public domain ptiches.com
Canstock.com/Kateryna-Kon

Kids.britannica.com/leaves

Lucifer;'s fall/ Gustave Dore

Dynamite – https/us/fotolia.com (Adobe Stock image)

NOAA.gov

https://oceanservice.noaa.gov

can stock photo/bluering, paulista

Rev. Dr. Naomi E. Peete is a Seattle, Washington transplant from Baltimore, Maryland. She is an ordained Minister, Motivational Speaker, Author, Science Educator, Science Communicator, and a Craft-Artist.

Dr. Peete is the founder of STEMWARE :Faith and Science Educational Materials. She is the proud mother of two sons: Herb and Maurice and one daughter Michelle; five grandchildren, and three great grands. Dr. Peete's ministry is to educate, empower, equip and encourage women and men towards applying Biblical Principles of Faith to daily practical Scientific application.
email: faithtoscience@gmail.com

www.ingramcontent.com/pod-product-compliance
Lightning Source LLC
Chambersburg PA
CBHW051246110526
44588CB00025B/2902